STUDIES IN ENGLISH LITERATURE No. 45

General Editor

David Daiches
Professor of English in the School of English
and American Studies, University of Sussex

W9-DIW-506

FOR JENNY

WEBSTER:
THE WHITE DEVIL

by

D. C. GUNBY

Lecturer in English,
The University of Canterbury,
New Zealand

EDWARD ARNOLD

© D. C. GUNBY, 1971

First published 1971 by
Edward Arnold (Publishers) Ltd.,
41 Maddox Street, London W1R 0AN

Cloth edition ISBN: 0 7131 5520 5
Paper edition ISBN: 0 7131 5563 9

All Rights Reserved. No part of this publication may be reproduced, stored in a retrieval system, or transmitted, in any form or by any means, electronic, mechanical, photocopying, recording or otherwise, without the prior permission of Edward Arnold (Publishers) Ltd.

NOTE

Quotations from and references to *The White Devil* are based on John Russell Brown's modern spelling text in the Revels Plays Series (2nd edition, 1966). I have, however, chosen not to follow Dr. Brown in altering 'Brachiano' to the technically correct 'Bracciano'. The anglicised form adopted by Webster has been so long accepted that any attempt now to 'rectify' the situation would seem pointless.

Quotations from plays by Webster other than *The White Devil* are from the old spelling text of F. L. Lucas in *The Complete Works of John Webster* (4 volumes, 1927), referred to in footnotes as 'Lucas, *Works*'.

Printed in Great Britain by
The Camelot Press Ltd, London and Southampton

General Preface

It has become increasingly clear in recent years that what both the advanced sixth-former and the university student need most by way of help in their literary studies are close critical analyses and evaluations of individual works. Generalisations about periods or authors, general chat about the Augustan Age or the Romantic Movement, have their uses; but all too often they provide merely the illusion of knowledge and understanding of literature. All too often students come up to the university under the impression that what is required of them in their English Literature courses is the referring of particular works to the appropriate generalisations about the writer or his period. Without taking up the anti-historical position of some of the American 'New Critics', we can nevertheless recognise the need for critical studies that concentrate on the work of literary art rather than on its historical background or cultural environment.

The present series is therefore designed to provide studies of individual plays, novels and groups of poems and essays, which are known to be widely studied in sixth forms and in universities. The emphasis is on clarification and evaluation; biographical and historical facts, while they may of course be referred to as helpful to an understanding of particular elements in a writer's work will be subordinated to critical discussion. What kind of work is this? What exactly goes on here? How good is this work, and why? These are the questions which each writer will try to answer.

DAVID DAICHES

Contents

I.	CRITICAL PERSPECTIVES	7
	The Dramatist and his Aims	7
	Truth of Argument	9
	Dignity of Persons	13
	Gravity and Height of Elocution	15
	Fullness and Frequency of Sentence	17
2.	THE WHITE DEVIL	21
	The Beginning	21
	The opening scene	21
	The lovers' meeting	23
	A family gathering	26
	The dumb shows	29
	The Middle	31
	The Trial	31
	Flamineo and Lodovico	35
	First moves towards revenge	36
	The lovers' quarrel	38
	The papal election	41
	The End	44
	Flamineo's fall	44
	The death of Brachiano	47
	The mad scene	50
	A false step	53
	Flamineo's mock death	54
	The final catastrophe	57
	FURTHER READING	62
	INDEX	63

1. Critical Perspectives

Few plays in English have generated greater critical disagreement than *The White Devil*. A recent editor, picking his way through a tangle of conflicting opinions, summarised the situation thus:

> Critical opinion cannot speak with certain or united voice about Webster's purposes; it has proved possible to talk of him as an old-fashioned moralist, as a sensationalist, as a social dramatist, as an imagist or dramatic symphonist, as a man fascinated by death, or a man halting between his inherited and his individual values.[1]

This diversity of critical approaches, although confusing, represents a challenge, testifying as it does to the depth and complexity of the play. In making our own way to the heart of *The White Devil*, we need constantly to remind ourselves of this complexity and to test the approach adopted here against those suggested by other critics.

The dramatist and his aims

The slowness and difficulty with which John Webster wrote were, it seems, common knowledge in the literary circles of Jacobean London. When, in 1617, one Henry Fitzjeffrey of Lincoln's Inn wished to attack Webster, he found the most telling satiric thrust to be a portrait of 'Crabbed (*Websterio*)/*The Play-wright, Cart-wright*' in the throes of composition:

> Was ever man so mangl'd with a *Poem*?
> See how he draws his mouth awry of late,
> How he scrubs: wrings his wrests: scratches his *Pate*.
> A *Midwife*! helpe! By his *Braines coitus*,
> Some *Centaure* strange: some huge *Bucephalus*,
> Or *Pallas* (sure) ingendred in his *Braine*,
> Strike, *Vulcan*, with thy hammer once againe.[2]

[1] John Russell Brown, in his introduction to the Revels *White Devil*, p. xliii.

[2] The attack is part of a poem, 'Notes from Black-Fryers', satirising various character-types in the audience of that theatre, printed in *Certain Elegies done by Sundry Excellent Wits*. The relevant section is given in full in Lucas, *Works*, I, 55.

It may be that *The White Devil* was written with even greater delibera-
tion than usual or simply that in this, his first major unaided venture,
Webster felt more vulnerable than in later years to criticism of his
artistic method. Whatever the reason, in the address to the reader with
which he prefaced the 1612 Quarto of the play, the dramatist devotes
some time to replying to 'those who report I was a long time in finishing
this tragedy'. 'I confess', he says,

> I do not write with a goose-quill, winged with two feathers, and if
> they will needs make it my fault, I must answer them with that of
> Euripides to Alcestides, a tragic writer: Alcestides objecting that
> Euripides had only in three days composed three verses, whereas
> himself had written three hundred: 'Thou tell'st truth,' (quoth he)
> 'but here's the difference,—thine shall be read for three days, whereas
> mine shall continue three ages.'

Webster provides further evidence of the scale against which he wished
to be measured when, at the end of the preface, he names those fellow
dramatists in whose company he would be read:

> Detraction is the sworn friend to ignorance: for mine own part I have
> ever truly cherish'd my good opinion of other men's worthy labours,
> especially of that full and height'ned style of Master Chapman, the
> labour'd and understanding works of Master Jonson: the no less
> worthy composures of the both worthily excellent Master Beaumont,
> and Master Fletcher: and lastly (without wrong last to be named)
> the right happy and copious industry of Master Shakespeare, Master
> Dekker, and Master Heywood, wishing what I write may be read
> by their light:

Though the list is catholic, setting essentially lightweight writers like
Dekker and Heywood cheek by jowl with Jonson and Shakespeare,
it makes Webster's critical preferences very plain. For though he
praises the ease and fluency of Shakespeare, Dekker and Heywood, and
offers a generalised tribute to Beaumont and Fletcher, he reserves pride
of place for the 'full and height'ned style of Master Chapman' and 'the
labour'd and understanding works of Master Jonson'.

In seeking to emulate these two writers in the creation of tragedy
learned and weighty enough to stand comparison with those of the
ancients, Webster recognised, as Jonson and Chapman did, the im-
possibility of adhering in every particular to the forms of Greek and
Roman tragedy. Borrowing at length, significantly enough, from

Jonson's preface to his first learned tragedy, *Sejanus* (1605), Webster explains this fact to his reader:

> If it be objected this is no true dramatic poem, I shall easily confess it,—*non potes in nugas dicere plura meas: ipso ego quam dixi,*—willingly, and not ignorantly, in this kind have I faulted: for should a man present to such an auditory, the most sententious tragedy that ever was written, observing all the critical laws, as height of style, and gravity of person, enrich it with the sententious *Chorus*, and as it were lifen death, in the passionate and weighty *Nuntius*: yet after all this divine rapture, *O dura messorum ilia*, the breath that comes from the uncapable multitude is able to poison it.

We may wonder, perhaps, to what extent a disclaimer of this kind demonstrated more the writer's competence in and familiarity with the formal austerities of classical drama than his desire to write according to this convention. But at the same time we must recognise that he is setting up the critical laws of the ancients as standards to be aspired to. The chorus and nuntius might have to be dispensed with, Jonson admitted in his preface to *Sejanus*, and also the 'strict Lawes of *Time*', but 'the other offices of a *Tragick* writer'—'truth of argument, dignity of persons, grauity and height of Elocution, fulnesse and frequencie of Sentence'—could—and should—be discharged.[3]

These 'offices', his preface implies, Webster too upheld. With them, therefore, an examination of *The White Devil* should begin.

Truth of argument

Although the copious marginal documentation of his two learned tragedies, *Sejanus* and *Catiline*, shows his respect for a detailed knowledge of the historical events he was dramatising, Jonson did not believe that 'truth of argument' meant simply 'historicity of argument'.[4] Like Chapman,[5] he believed that

> hee is call'd a *Poet*, not hee which writeth in measure only; but that fayneth and formeth a fable, and writes things like the Truth. For, the Fable and Fiction is (as it were) the forme and Soule of any Poeticall work, or *Poeme*.[6]

[3] 'To the Readers', in *The Works of Ben Jonson*, ed. C. H. Herford and P. Simpson, 10 vols. (Oxford, 1925–52), IV, 350.

As a historian Jonson sought to remain true to his sources. As a poet and dramatist, he knew that he was entitled to shape a historical argument, providing it with a form and unity which, merely re-told, it would not possess.

The historical facts which lie behind *The White Devil* are these. Vittoria Accoramboni was born at Gubbio, a small town in the Apennines, on 15 February 1557. The family was poor, though of good standing, and Vittoria, as one of eleven children, came to realise that her future prosperity depended upon her beauty, which was considerable. Her mother, who was of the same opinion, took her to Rome, where she met, fell in love with, and (in June 1573) was married to Francesco Peretti, a nephew of Cardinal Montalto. At first all went well, but Vittoria was gay and given to extravagance, while Francesco was very much under the thumb of his stern and parsimonious uncle, and trouble developed to a point at which Vittoria began looking for a wealthier protector. In 1580 she found one (perhaps through the agency of her brother, Marcello, then the Duke's chamberlain) in Paolo Giordano Orsini, Duke of Bracciano.

Bracciano had been married in 1558 to Isabella de Medici, by whom he had had three children, including, in 1572, a son and heir, Virginio. In 1576, however, he had discovered that Isabella had a lover, a distant relative of his named Troilo Orsini, and she had died in suspicious circumstances, probably strangled by Bracciano himself. In 1581 he took steps to provide as conveniently for the freedom of Vittoria, by having Peretti murdered in the street. Within a fortnight Bracciano and Vittoria were married in secret.

The next four years the couple spent trying to reverse or evade an order from the Pope, Gregory XIII, that they should separate. Vittoria herself spent a period in Castel St. Angelo, during which, temporarily abandoned by Bracciano, she tried unsuccessfully to commit suicide. Upon her release, however, the liaison was resumed, and in October

4 See J. A. Bryant Jnr., 'The Significance of Ben Jonson's First Requirement for Tragedy: "Truth of Argument"', *Studies in Philology*, XLIX (1952), 195–213.

5 See Chapman's dedicatory epistle to *The Revenge of Bussy d'Ambois* (1613), where he remarks: 'And for the autentical truth of either person or action, who (worth the respecting) will expect it in a poem, whose subject is not truth, but things like truth?' *The Plays of George Chapman*, ed. T. M. Parrott (New York, 1961), *The Tragedies*, Vol. I, p. 77.

6 Herford and Simpson, *Works*, VIII, 635.

1583 the couple were married a second time, in public at Bracciano. Just as a further enforced separation seemed inevitable Pope Gregory died. During the interregnum Bracciano, having secured the opinion of pliant theologians that the prohibitions imposed by the previous Pope had died with him, married Vittoria a third time. Within hours their arch-enemy, Cardinal Montalto, was proclaimed Pope, taking the title of Sixtus V.

Curiously enough the new Pope did not exact the vengeance that might have been expected, though they continued to suffer his severe disfavour. Accordingly the Duke and his wife left Rome, travelling first to Venice, then Padua, and finally, on account of his deteriorating health, to Salo on Lake Garda. There, on 13 November 1585, he died. Vittoria, after an outburst of despair in which she tried to shoot herself, settled down to enjoy her very comfortable widowhood, having been lavishly provided for in Bracciano's will. This very lavishness was, however, her undoing, for the Medici relatives of Bracciano's first wife became alarmed at the inroads being made upon the inheritance of the Duke's heir, Virginio. After seeking to reach a compromise, which Vittoria refused, they decided to have her murdered. The task was undertaken by a kinsman and former confidant of Bracciano, Lodovico Orsini, who invaded her palace at the head of a band of followers, and killed both Vittoria and her young brother Flamineo. Four days later (on 27 December 1585) Lodovico, having been found guilty by the authorities in Padua, was executed. Within the next few days many of his followers suffered the same fate.

That the facts of history and Webster's dramatisation of them differ in many respects is at once apparent. There are, firstly, numerous changes of name: Francesco Peretti, for example, becomes Camillo, while his uncle, Cardinal Montalto, is renamed Monticelso. Secondly, there are changes of role. Historically, both Isabella de Medici and Vittoria's mother were less than admirable: Webster makes them both virtuous. Lastly, there are alterations to the pattern of events. Historically, Isabella's death had nothing to do with Bracciano's love for Vittoria, but took place four years prior to their first meeting. The manner of Bracciano's death too is altered. In the play he is poisoned: in fact he died a natural death; a victim of his obesity. Nor is there historical warrant for Flamineo's cowardly murder of Marcello, or Cornelia's madness, while Lodovico's capture was actually accomplished only after a regular siege of the palace in which he had taken refuge.

For these departures from history two explanations are possible. The first is that the sources of Webster's information were themselves inaccurate. The second is that he deliberately altered the facts to meet his artistic requirements.

What we know of the sources suggests that they were, to some extent, responsible for Webster's divergences from historical fact. If Dr. Gunnar Boklund is right, then Webster's primary source was one of a regular series of newsletters sent to the Fugger banking family in Augsburg by one of its many Italian agents.[7] From this letter he would have gathered not only the broad outlines of the whole affair, but also several major departures from fact: that Isabella was still alive when Bracciano met Vittoria; that the Duke's son was named Giovanni; that Lodovico himself stabbed Vittoria; and that the Pope took no further part in the pursuit of Vittoria after Bracciano's death. He would also have learned that 'foul play was suspected' over the death of Bracciano. The Fugger newsletter was certainly not Webster's only source, however. The manner in which Brachiano is poisoned is probably taken from Boaistuau's *Theatrum Mundi*, where we learn of a certain Florentine knight who 'died suddenly' after his helmet was poisoned during a tournament, while the behaviour of the two 'friars' at the bedside of the dying man is borrowed from Erasmus' colloquy, *Funus*. For the details of the conclave scene two sources are possible. The less likely is John Florio's *A Letter Lately Written from Rome* (1585), which recounts the death of Gregory XIII and the election of Sixtus V. The other is Hierome Bignon's *A Brief, but an Effectuall Treatise of the Election of Popes* (1605), which, though dealing with the election of Leo II in 1605, relates more closely to the scene in *The White Devil*.

Even taking into account all the proven inaccuracies of source, however, we are left with a considerable number of changes which must, unless a hitherto undiscovered source comes to light, be taken as Webster's own. Some of these we may put down to his desire to tighten the structure of his digressive and episodic tale. The capture of Lodovico and his accomplices immediately after the murders achieves this end. So, too, does the conflation, in the career of Webster's Flamineo, of aspects of the lives of two of Vittoria's brothers; the villainous Marcello, and Flamineo, the innocent sufferer in the final calamity. Other changes are dictated by Webster's dramatic sense. Vittoria married to the young Peretti would have to be unequivocally condemned for her behaviour

[7] *The Sources of The White Devil* (Uppsala, 1957), pp. 122–32.

towards her husband: Vittoria married to Camillo may be felt to have some cause for dissatisfaction, if not for inciting her lover to murder him. Similarly, the great trial scene (III, ii), though without warrant in history, is essential to the play: the lingering incarceration which Vittoria in fact suffered formed no workable basis for dramatic action of the kind Webster sought.

Finally, the didactic purpose in some of Webster's alterations, sometimes secondary to his dramatic or aesthetic motives and sometimes paramount, cannot be ignored. The creation of Marcello and the unhistorical virtues of Cornelia and Isabella are examples of this didactic purpose: like Marcello, the two women are needed as examples of virtue by which others may be measured. There are didactic implications, too, in the manner of Brachiano's death, in the creation of Zanche, in Francisco's choice of disguise, and in the grotesque mock-death which Flamineo stages at the beginning of the final scene. All of these changes reinforce the meaning which Webster perceived in the chronicle-like formlessness of the original narrative, a meaning which seemed to him to justify his reshaping of the facts of history in pursuit of 'truth of argument'.

Dignity of persons

The 'dignity of persons' which Jonson lists among the 'offices of a Tragick writer', and whose value Webster also recognised, is an expression of the important Renaissance critical concept of decorum. The principles of universality and verisimilitude upon which this concept chiefly relied had their origin in Aristotle's four basic requirements for characterisation: that characters should be good; that they should be drawn with propriety (that is, true to type); that they should be true to life; and that they should be self-consistent.[8] The reductio ad absurdum of these general and undogmatic observations was the elaborate critical structure developed chiefly by Italian theorists whose concern was the detailed prescription of the proper traits for every character-type in the dramatist's range.

Both as dramatist and as critic, Jonson rejected such prescriptions. 'I am not of that opinion', he remarks in Discoveries, 'to conclude a Poets liberty within the narrowe limits of lawes, which either the

[8] See J. E. Spingarn, A History of Literary Criticism in the Renaissance (New York, 1924), pp. 85–9.

Grammarians, or *Philosophers* prescribe. For, before they found out those Lawes, there were many excellent Poets, that fulfill'd them.'[9] He did not abandon the concept of decorum, but, holding that 'rules are ever of lesse force, and valew, then experiments'[10] he chose to rely on his own experience and judgement rather than theoretical prescriptions.

Webster, as *The White Devil* proves, also combines adherence to critical precepts with a pragmatic approach to their application. In striving for what he calls 'gravity of person' he creates characters sufficiently typical to satisfy the requirements of decorum, yet at the same time distinctively individual. Brachiano and Francisco, for example, are both Dukes, and both portrayed as such. Yet while sharing that dignity of mien and awareness of rank which decorum demanded of an aristocrat, they differ quite radically in other respects. Brachiano is brave, as a Duke should be (cowardice being allowed only among the lower orders of society), but his courage is of the noisy, obvious kind, and accompanied by a tendency to bully and bluster. Francisco, on the other hand, is devious, and chooses to undermine his opponent rather than attack him openly. In part such differences too can be attributed to decorum, which demands that men should be shown as old or young, and not as inhabitants of the no-man's-land of middle age, so that Webster varies history to make Brachiano a young man, subject to the fiery impetuosity of the typical youth, and his brother-in-law and contemporary, Francisco, old and experienced. Other influences can be traced, however, in the individualisation of Webster's characters. One is humour psychology, with its definition of four basic personality types reinforcing the concept of the typical inherent in the idea of decorum. Another is the native tradition in English drama, the morality play, which while dealing basically in types of vice and virtue, added individual and highly realistic detail in the interests of immediacy. In Brachiano, therefore, the attributes of the choleric man are added to those of the young Duke, while Francisco is not merely an old Duke, but also phlegmatic in temperament and a descendant of the morality vice.

The other major characters exhibit the same combination of the typical and the individual. Monticelso is a Cardinal, sharing characteristics with the princes of the Church found in *The Duchess of Malfi*, Middleton's *Women Beware Women*, and Shirley's *The Cardinal*. Yet

9 Herford and Simpson, *Works*, VIII, 641.
10 Ibid., VIII, 617.

he holds our interest as a individual, a man who, by contrast with Francisco, begins by seeking revenge but ends by abjuring it. Isabella, for her part, is type-cast as the noble and faithful wife, but individualised as more than this, while in Giovanni sufficient is added to the stock portrait of the child prince to make him one of the more attractive of the children in Jacobean drama. Lodovico, like Bosola after him, is in some respects a reluctant villain, recognising the claims of morality even as he flouts them.

Decorum demanded a strict division between the characters of one social class and another. In Marcello and Cornelia, types of the honest soldier and virtuous mother, we find this class distinction clearly observed. With Flamineo, the university-educated secretary, it is less clear-cut, though we are kept aware of the differences in social standing between him and his employer as well as, in a more subtle way, between him and his counterpart in the malcontent tradition, Lodovico. In Vittoria, however, social distinctions are thoroughly blurred. One minute vulgarly vituperative, she can in the next display courage, wit and eloquence equalling (and in some ways surpassing) the aristocratic magnificence of Brachiano, Francisco and Monticelso. In so doing, of course, she also violates another of decorum's basic tenets. Aristotle observed that 'There is a type of manly valour; but valour in a woman, or unscrupulous cleverness, is inappropriate.' Vittoria, who admits that in self-defence she is forced to 'personate masculine virtue', combines masculine traits and feminine in a way which blatantly violates the distinctions demanded between the sexes. This blurring of accepted canons might support Ian Jack's complaint that Webster commits an 'artistic insincerity' in making the guilty Vittoria seem innocent.[11] In fact it not only makes Vittoria one of the most complex and intriguing of Jacobean heroines, but also serves to warn us against the combination of attractiveness and criminality which the epithet 'white devil' comprehends.

Gravity and height of Elocution

Renaissance man inherited a tradition which placed a high value on the art of rhetoric and ascribed a deep significance to language. 'No glasse', says Jonson in *Discoveries*,

[11] 'The Case of John Webster', *Scrutiny*, XVI (1949), 38–43.

renders a mans forme, or likenesse, so true as his speech. Nay, it is
likened to a man; and as we consider feature, and composition in a
man; so words in Language: in the greatnesse, aptnesse, sound,
structure, and harmony of it.[12]

It is not surprising, therefore, to find the doctrine of decorum extended
to cover what a man says as well as how he acts, or to find theorists
like Minturno prescribing in detail what is appropriate, both in manner
and in matter, in the speech of the different character-types. In deter-
mining this, however, critics were guided not only by the character and
status of the speaker, but also by the genre to which the work in which
he appeared belongs. Confusing what in Aristotle is an ethical distinction
between men 'above our own level of goodness, or beneath it, or
just as we are', the Italian theorists determined that tragedy, as the
highest of the forms of scenic (or dramatic) poetry, demanded the
depiction of persons of noble birth. To do justice to this combination
of noble themes and aristocratic characters, decorum and the theory
of genres alike demanded an 'elevated' style, *sublime* or *altisonum*.

While generally cavalier in their attitude to other rules governing the
'correct' writing of tragedy, English dramatists agreed that, for the
tragic protagonists at least, it was necessary to achieve what Jonson
calls 'gravity and height of elocution' and Webster 'height of style'.
In search of this goal, Webster pursued—to a degree unequalled, so far
as is known, by any other dramatist of the time—a policy of literary
borrowing.[13]

The knowledge that more than three-quarters of all that Webster
wrote was borrowed from the works of others comes as a shock in an
age critical of plagiarism. To the Jacobean, however, reared in a rhetorical
tradition which commended 'imitation', borrowing was to be censured
only when, as with Thomas Lodge, it took the form of large-scale
theft.[14] For the rest,

this is one kinde of fruit gotten by readinge, that a man may imitate
that which he lyketh and alloweth in others, and such speciall poyntes

[12] Herford and Simpson, *Works*, VIII, 625.
[13] See R. W. Dent, *John Webster's Borrowing* (Berkeley, 1960), for a
full study of this aspect of Webster's creativity.
[14] Lodge was capable of 'borrowing' as much as 'twenty pages at a
stretch'. See Alice Walker, 'The Reading of an Elizabethan: Some Sources
of the Prose Pamphlets of Thomas Lodge', *Review of English Studies*,
VIII (1932), 265.

and sayinges as hee is especially delighted & in loue withall, by apt and fitte deriuation maye wrest to serue his owne turne and purpose.[15]

The style which Webster forges by making his borrowings 'serue his owne turne and purpose' reflects to some extent the method of composition. Tense and tightly-knit, the speeches present themselves not as sustained poetic utterances (there are only a handful of these, all formalised in some way, in the entire play), but as a series of phrases or fragments of sense. The effect, which constant variations in the pace and tone of the verse reinforce, is of a nervous and at times disjunctive movement, with almost epigrammatic intensity of significance. Often elliptical in grammar and syntax, intricate in its shifts of thought and feeling, and full of puns and quibbles, Webster's language demands close and constant attention. This it repays by its richness and diversity, its subtle ironies and moments of utter simplicity, and its ability to convey nuances of character. It repays us, above all, in its imagery, which, as in Flamineo's warning to Marcello, 'When age shall turn thee/White as a blooming hawthorn', reveals that quality of unexpectedness, that capacity to relate the apparently unrelated or invert accepted metaphoric associations, which is characteristically metaphysical. It is paradoxical that, admiring Jonson and Chapman, and striving to emulate their achievements in the tragic mode, Webster developed an 'elevated' style which has little in common with theirs, but much with the poetry of John Donne.

Fullness and frequency of sentence

To sixteenth-century men, the chief function of literature was didactic. Among Italian critics, only Castelvetro disagreed, claiming that 'poetry was invented exclusively to delight and give recreation'.[16] Prudently, in opposing a generally held critical 'truth', he went to Aristotle for his defence:

> Those who insist that poetry was invented mainly to profit, or to profit and delight together, let them beware lest they oppose the authority of Aristotle, who . . . seems to assign nothing but pleasure to it; and if, indeed, he concedes some utility to it, he concedes it accidentally, as is the case with the purgation of fear and of pity by means of tragedy.[17]

[15] Franciscus Patricius, *A Morale Methode of ciuile Policie*, trans. Robinson (1576), sigs. a1–a1v.
[16] See Bernard Weinberg, *A History of Literary Criticism in the Italian Renaissance*, 2 vols. (Chicago, 1961), I, 504.
[17] Ibid., I, 506.

Bw

Not unexpectedly, orthodox theorists also cited Aristotle, linking his concept of *catharsis* and the demand for 'goodness' among the requisites for character with Horace's *prodesse* and *utile* and the Platonic notion of utility, to produce a case for the primacy of instruction over delight. To the modern mind, this argument seems highly suspect, involving a distortion of Aristotle's meaning, as well as a highly selective reading of Horace's description of the role of the poet as 'aut prodesse . . . aut delectare . . . aut simul et iucunda et idonea dicere vitae' (*either* to profit *or* to delight *or* to utter words at once both pleasing and helpful to life). To the sixteenth-century writer or critic, however, steeped in a medieval Christian tradition as well as a classical pagan one, it seemed both right and natural that poetry should assume the function of moral philosophy, just as it seemed logical to derive from Aristotle's theories a view of tragedy as moralistic as this of Minturno's:

> the tragic poet . . . sets before us the characters . . . of men who seem in the eyes of other men to be outstanding for their dignity, power, and indeed every favour of fortune, and nevertheless sink to extreme unhappiness because of some human error. This he does so that we may see that no trust is to be put in the smooth course of events, that there is nothing on earth so lasting and stable that it cannot fall and die, nothing so firm and strong that it cannot be overthrown, nothing so happy and exalted that it cannot be made unhappy and brought low; and so that when we contemplate so great a change of fortune in others, we may take heed lest misfortunes come to us against our hope and against our expectation, and so that when they do happen—since things of this sort are wont to happen to men—we may bear them with an unruffled soul.[18]

In emphasising these lessons, *sententiae* or generalised moral comments were assigned a major role. All the English dramatists used them: some, like Fletcher, in a perfunctory and extraneous fashion; others, like Marston, Chapman and Jonson, as an integral part of the moral structure of their plays. No one, however, makes more frequent use of the 'sentence', or assigns it a more important role, than Webster. Unable, as he tells us in his prefatory address, to 'enrich' *The White Devil* with a 'sententious *Chorus*' because of 'the uncapable multitude', he follows

[18] Ibid., II, 738. Chapman provides an English equivalent when he remarks, in the preface to *The Revenge of Bussy d'Ambois*: 'material instruction, elegant and sententious excitation to virtue, and deflection from her contrary, [are] the soul, limbs, and limits of an authentical tragedy'. *The Tragedies*, I, 77.

the next best course, and distributes his choric commentary amongst the leading characters.

In the Quarto of 1612 these choric statements are often distinguished typographically, as at IV, ii, 246–7 or V, vi, 250–4. Just as often, however, a maxim will appear (because, it seems, of the differing habits of the two compositors employed in setting the play)[19] without typographical indication. In I, i, for example, at least seven passages warrant consideration as *sententiae*, including the final couplet:

> Great men sell sheep, thus to be cut in pieces,
> When first they have shorn them bare and sold their fleeces.
>
> (I, i, 62–3)

Marked or unmarked, however, the maxims scattered so liberally throughout *The White Devil* play an important part in forming and controlling our response to the action.

A similar effect is achieved through the use of the tale, examples of which occur in *The White Devil* at II, i, 335–56 and IV, ii, 222–35. Until recently, critics generally deplored Webster's use of these set-pieces, joining Rupert Brooke in labelling them 'long-winded, irrelevant, and fantastically unrealistic'.[20] Recognition that the tales are not irrelevant, but bear strongly upon the events they interrupt, has brought with it a better understanding of Webster's aims, and an awareness that only through extensive stylisation can he create the extra-dramatic interludes necessary for chorically directed reflection.

What is the audience to reflect upon? What are the lessons which *The White Devil* seeks to convey? In answering we must, I think, distinguish between (without separating) two levels of didactic intention: the immediate and the ultimate. On the immediate level, the play has much to say about the perils of court life, and the illusory nature of greatness. The reader is to learn, in Webster's own words, of 'courtly reward and punishment', and having discovered that 'Glories, like glow-worms, afar off shine bright/But look'd to near, have neither heat nor light', to conclude, with Vittoria: 'O happy they that never saw the court,/ Nor ever knew great man but by report'. More importantly, he is to recognise the futility of the parasite's frenzied search for advancement, and acknowledge, as Flamineo belatedly does, that 'rest breeds rest, where all seek pain by pain'.

---

[19] See Brown, Revels *White Devil*, pp. lxix–lxx.
[20] *John Webster and the Elizabethan Drama* (1916), p. 130.

Underlying these lessons are others more universal in significance. 'While we look up to heaven we confound/Knowledge with knowledge', says the dying Flamineo. Webster is at pains to prevent his reader making a similar mistake by stressing the indivisibility of the material and the spiritual, and placing the everyday in an eternal perspective. Life and death, heaven and hell, salvation and damnation; these form the frame of reference within which Webster demonstrates the workings of a pattern of retribution as apt as it is inexorable, and proves that, despite the sufferings of the virtuous, good must eventually triumph over evil.

Described thus, *The White Devil* might be taken for a medieval morality play, austere in form, simplistic in its underlying assumptions, and single-minded in its presentation of a thesis. The commentary which follows is intended to show that it is, in fact, none of these things; that despite the Augustinian rigour of the beliefs upon which it is founded, the play is rich in character and incident, subtly planned and executed, and, as the critical conflicts over its meaning prove, far from obvious. Nor does this imply a conflict between the play's meaning and its form. On the contrary, the very richness of *The White Devil* reinforces its message. Vittoria is a white devil, but she is also a brilliant and resourceful woman, beautiful, courageous and highly intelligent, and we cannot help responding to her with some sympathy and warmth. In doing so we are not only paying tribute to Webster's ability to create a living character, but also demonstrating the force of his argument by following, to some extent, in the footsteps of Brachiano. Adapting Marshall McLuhan's famous phrase, we might say that in *The White Devil* the medium is part of the message.

2. *The White Devil*

With the simplicity of brilliance, Aristotle observed that a properly constructed play should possess a clearly defined beginning, middle and end. The critics of the Italian Renaissance, seeking to explain the predominance of the five-act structure in contemporary drama, gradually developed a philosophical justification for a five part division:

> . . . to all wise men this number seemed perfect: and rightfully so, since, just as in life, so in every complete human action we see the beginning, the increase, the climax, the decline, and the end. And I believe that Aristotle intended that all these parts should be required in that single action which the poet undertakes to describe, so that it may be whole and perfect and of a proper magnitude.[1]

Minturno's theory, however, when applied to *The White Devil*, is less useful than Aristotle's much simpler requirement. For though the play is divided into the traditional five acts, it cannot be claimed that these correspond to any meaningful degree to Minturno's five parts. Act One should, according to Minturno, be devoted to the beginning, or exposition. Yet I, ii, after completing the beginning of the action, sets us well on the way into the increase. In the same way, though the climax begins with III, i, the decline might be said to begin either with III, iii, or IV, i, and to end either with V, ii, or (depending on the emphasis one places upon Brachiano's role) with V, v.

If instead we follow Aristotle and take Acts I and II to be the beginning, Acts III and IV the middle, and Act V the ending, we have a useful framework within which to make a detailed study of *The White Devil*.

THE BEGINNING

The opening scene

The first scene of *The White Devil* is a masterly piece of exposition.

[1] Quoted by Weinberg in *A History of Literary Criticism in the Italian Renaissance*, II, 757.

Opening with an arresting suddenness and force, it lays before us all the information necessary to an understanding of the action.

We learn first of Lodovico, of his banishment, and of 'certain murders here in Rome,/Bloody and full of horror' (I, i, 31–2) which are the reason for it. His friends, Gasparo and Antonelli, in seeking to convince him that he is 'justly doom'd', detail the stages whereby he has sunk from being a wealthy landowner to a penniless adventurer, forced to eke out a living by an uncertain dependence on others. Their catalogue is presented in the form of a highly stylised duologue, such as Webster is fond of using at times like this. Its effect is choric, carrying a special weight of emphasis. Within twenty lines we have been supplied with all the information we need to understand Lodovico's character and background.

In his cynicism, Lodovico jeers at the law for not having had him executed for murder. Gasparo explains with apparent sincerity that 'the law doth sometimes mediate, thinks it good/Not ever to steep violent sins in blood' (34–5). Lodovico, however, is unmoved, and bitterly compares his lot with that of another more influential transgressor:

> So,—but I wonder then some great men scape
> This banishment,—there's Paolo Giordano Orsini,
> The Duke of Brachiano, now lives in Rome,
> And by close pandarism seeks to prostitute
> The honour of Vittoria Corombona,—
> Vittoria, she that might have got my pardon
> For one kiss to the duke. (I, i, 38–44)

In making this comparison, Lodovico not only unobtrusively furthers the exposition, but also emphasises the similarity of the Duke's moral standing to his own, a verdict which subsequent events confirm. We should note, however, that Vittoria is not so precisely placed. We are told that Brachiano is seeking to seduce her: it is not clear whether she is responding favourably or not. The ambiguities with which Webster is constantly presenting us in his portrayal of the white devil have begun.

Many of Lodovico's comments throughout the play have a bearing on the main action. His bitter observation about 'Courtly reward,/And punishment', for instance, highlights what is to be a major theme, affecting not only himself and his friends, but also his opponents, Vittoria and Flamineo. They, like him, will learn the deeper implications of his lighthearted if cynical exchange with Gasparo:

Gasp.   You term those enemies
  Are men of princely rank.
Lod.   O I pray for them.
  The violent thunder is adored by those
  Are pash'd in pieces by it. (I, i, 9–12)

Equally all will come to share Lodovico's bitter summary of 'the world's alms':

  Great men sell sheep, thus to be cut in pieces,
  When first they have shorn them bare and sold their fleeces.
                                       (I, i, 62–3)

Other remarks, too, have a more general application than is at first apparent. Though the play as a whole will disprove the view that Fortune dominates men's lives, there will be seen to be some truth in Lodovico's assertion that the rewards doled out to men, little by little, are at last taken away 'all at one swoop'. Finally, we will discover how ironic is Lodovico's envy of the great man's ability to evade punishment. As Brachiano's death will show, in the world of *The White Devil* no one is exempt from the workings of retribution.

The lovers' meeting

The first scene ends as dramatically as it began, with a flourish of trumpets. Its effect is two-fold. On the one hand, by causing Lodovico and his confederates to disperse, it emphasises the clandestine nature of the meeting that has just taken place. On the other it heightens our expectations concerning what is to come. Vittoria sweeps on, dressed in white, amid a blaze of torches. Greeting Brachiano, she calls for more lights, and then sweeps off, with Camillo in silent attendance. Brachiano then turns to Flamineo who, as they begin plotting, orders the attendants to extinguish their torches and depart; this return to the gloom in which Lodovico and his friends met recalls the parallels established earlier. All the foreboding of this discussion of ways of duping Camillo and satisfying Brachiano's passion for Vittoria is contained in the Duke's comment, 'Quite lost Flamineo' (I, ii, 3).

The conversation which ensues clearly delineates the characters of the Duke and his secretary. Brachiano is here the traditional lover, at once happy and eager, anxious and self-deprecatory. As such he is very much in the hands of Flamineo, who allows his gross and cynical wit to play upon every aspect of the situation. Feminine modesty he sees as 'but the superficies of lust', and demands to know why ladies should 'blush to hear that nam'd, which they do not fear to handle?' Love itself is compared to 'a summer bird-cage in a garden,—the birds that are without, despair to get in, and the birds that are within despair and are in a consumption for fear they shall never get out' (I, ii, 43–6). His remarks are amusing, but Flamineo also has a role to play in conditioning our response to Brachiano and his love for Vittoria. Throughout the passage, in fact, there is an ironic counterpointing of Flamineo's grossness and cynicism against the conventional terminology of the noble lover, which underlines the essential sordidness of the action.

The return of Camillo presents Flamineo with a further opportunity for the exercise of his wit. In responding with some very much less subtle word-play upon the game of bowls as a metaphor for love-making, Camillo makes his fear of cuckoldry plain. Seizing on this, Flamineo puts into effect his plan for getting rid of Camillo so that Vittoria and Brachiano may meet undisturbed. In general terms he is no doubt right in claiming that 'women are more willingly and more gloriously chaste, when they are least restrained of their liberty'. But there is a distinct double-edge to the discussion of jealousy which follows, and Flamineo's remark, 'they that have the yellow jaundice, think all objects they look on to be yellow', serves as an apt description of his own distorted views of virtue and vice.

The entry of Vittoria enables Flamineo to complete the duping of Camillo. Using the quibble and the aside to inform her and us of what is really intended, he deludes Camillo into believing that by refusing to sleep with Vittoria, he will bring her to a more wifely obedience. Again Flamineo's verbal dexterity works as much against the cause he is advocating as for it. From line 145 he is using the term 'my lord' ambiguously, meaning Brachiano, but appearing to refer to Camillo. The ambiguity carries over into Flamineo's vision of Vittoria's future happiness (I, ii, 156–8). For the lovers—and for Flamineo himself—happiness will prove as illusory as it does for Camillo. Like Camillo, they will entangle themselves in their own work 'like a silkworm'.

With the departure of Camillo and the re-entry of Brachiano, the scene takes a new turn. While Brachiano expresses the traditional lover's wish that time might stand still, Flamineo bluntly encourages his sister to respond, crudely comparing her situation with that of a dog let loose at midnight. This duality of tone and mood is to be present at

every one of the lovers' encounters. We never see them alone: Flamineo
is always there, commenting on the action in a manner as debased as it
is witty. Because of this there is never any danger that we will take
Vittoria and Brachiano at their own valuation, or fail to criticise as we
admire.

There is another factor, too, preventing an uncritical response to
the lovers: the presence of Cornelia. Entering, significantly enough,
at the very moment when Zanche is spreading a rug and cushions for
the lovers to recline on, she represents from the first both a threat and
a reproach. Hers is the voice of orthodox morality.

Brachiano's first speech to Vittoria ends in supplication:

> Loose me not madam, for if you forego me
> I am lost eternally. (I, ii, 207–8)

The phrase recalls the Duke's opening remark to Flamineo: the pun
underlines the deeper significance of the lover's conceits which follow.
Brachiano sees Vittoria as 'a sweet physician' because 'in the way of
pity' she wishes him 'heart-whole'. In fact, however, the 'loathed
cruelty' she rejects would do more for his 'credit', and hers, than her
mercy.

The opening pleasantries concluded with a highly suggestive exchange
of 'jewels', Vittoria quickly consolidates her hold on Brachiano. She
conveys through the 'dream' of the yew-tree her fears that Camillo
and Brachiano's Duchess, Isabella, will intervene to prevent their
happiness. Flamineo's cynical response carries with it sinister implications:

> Excellent devil.
> She hath taught him in a dream
> To make away his duchess and her husband. (I, ii, 256–8)

Brachiano interprets the dream exactly as he is meant to, promising
to protect Vittoria and to set her 'above law and above scandal'. Though
time is needed for the full irony in this promise to be revealed, its empti-
ness is immediately made apparent by Cornelia's denunciation and
prophecy of disaster. And as she informs them of the arrival of Isabella
in Rome, scandal at least seems very near.

The lovers' responses to Cornelia's denunciation differ greatly.
Brachiano blusters angrily, indifferent, so it seems, to issues of morality.
Vittoria, however, is shaken by her mother's words and, kneeling, tries
to excuse her behaviour. The action reminds us, ironically, of the dutiful

child claiming a parent's blessing. The irony is underlined when Cornelia
too kneels, to pronounce a curse:

> I will join with thee,
> To the most woeful end e'er mother kneel'd,—
> If thou dishonour thus thy husband's bed,
> Be thy life short as are the funeral tears
> In great men's,—
> *Brac.*   Fie, fie, the woman's mad.
> *Cor.* Be thy act Judas-like—betray in kissing,
> May'st thou be envied during his short breath,
> And pitied like a wretch after his death.
> *Vit.* O me accurst. (I, ii, 293–301)

As events prove, the curse is prophetic. Brachiano's life will be short,
even shorter than Vittoria's, and the tears shed over him will be perfunctory in the extreme. Moreover, he will, like Judas, betray with
kisses those he loves or has loved, and finally pay, like Judas, for his
betrayals.

Cornelia's curse concludes the lovers' tryst. Vittoria flees from the
room, and Brachiano, after ordering Flamineo to summon Doctor Julio
and, angrily warning Cornelia that she will be 'the cause of all ensuing
harm', departs also. This leaves Cornelia to face her son, who attacks
her bitterly for damaging his chances of preferment. Cornelia defends
herself with what to her is a rhetorical question, 'What? because we are
poor,/Shall we be vicious?' but Flamineo contemptuously brushes aside
the claims of morality, by reminding her that the parasite cannot afford
scruples.

A family gathering

The first ten lines of II, i provide further proof of Webster's gift for
exposition. Not pausing to refer to the Cardinal, whose attire is self-
explanatory, or to explain Marcello's role, which is clearly that of a
subordinate, he indicates that Isabella and Francisco are brother and
sister, that she is Brachiano's Duchess, and that the boy, not yet identified
by name, is their son. A second group of ten lines then establishes Isabella's gentle and loving nature, her capacity for forgiveness, and her
simple trust that love will be sufficient to keep Brachiano 'chaste from
an infected straying'.

The discord which threatens with the entry of the Duke is averted by the Cardinal's entreaty that he 'forego all passion/Which may be rais'd by my free discourse'. Brachiano's reply, 'As silent as i'th' church', is ironically apt, for Monticelso's 'discourse' takes the form of a sermon, including first compliments, then moral exhortations, and finally a warning of the sorrows of remorse. The reproof strains Brachiano's limited self-control. The less temperate strictures of Francisco break it, and the discussion degenerates into a slanging-match. Just when physical violence seems certain, however, Monticelso intervenes and, taking advantage of the re-entry of Giovanni, he restores a semblance of amity.

Briefly, while Giovanni charms his father and uncle with his precocity, this amity seems to grow, and Brachiano and Francisco shake hands, affirming a friendship 'like bones which broke in sunder and well set/ Knit the more strongly'. Once Brachiano and Isabella are left alone, however, it emerges that the Duke has no desire for a reconciliation. By now hypersensitive to criticism, he misinterprets a general observation that 'the oftener that we cast our reckonings up,/Our sleeps will be the sounder', and angrily orders her to leave. Timidly, she begs a kiss, but is repulsed. Trying again to demonstrate her love, she is brushed aside with the brutal comment:

> O your breath!
> Out upon sweet meats, and continued physic!
> The plague is in them. (II, i, 163–5)

All her efforts at conciliation are vain, for Brachiano labels her love 'dissemblance', and imputes her coming to Rome to base motives. Angrily reviling Francisco, who 'first made this match', he curses 'the priest/That sang the wedding mass, and even my issue'.

With this curse, the scene enters a new and highly stylised phase: one designed to present, in symbolic terms, the full implications, moral and religious, personal and social, of Brachiano's rejection of Isabella. This is done through what one critic has called 'inverted rituals', through the reversal of the ceremonies of betrothal and marriage which had made the two man and wife.[2] Hence we find Brachiano's private vow of separation (II, i, 192–8), followed, when Francisco, Monticelso, Marcello and Flamineo return, by Isabella's 'public' repudiation, in terms which are a reversal of the pledge made at their betrothal:

---

[2] James R. Hurt, 'Inverted Rituals in Webster's *The White Devil*', *Journal of English and Germanic Philology*, LXI (1962), 42–7.

> *Isa.*   Brother draw near, and my lord cardinal,—
>   Sir, let me borrow of you but one kiss,
>   Henceforth I'll never lie with you, by this,
>   This wedding-ring.
> *Fran.*   How? ne'er more lie with him?—
> *Isa.*   And this divorce shall be as truly kept,
>   As if in thronged court, a thousand ears
>   Had heard it, and a thousand lawyers' hands
>   Seal'd to the separation. (II, i, 252–9)

That it is Isabella who performs the public ceremony, and so takes upon herself the blame for the separation, is significant in a number of ways. On the personal level her act of self-sacrifice demonstrates her strength, and at the same time Brachiano's weakness. Symbolically, too, it is important. The kiss which seals the formal act of separation is, on Brachiano's part, a symbol of the betrayal which Cornelia foretold, yet for Isabella it represents precisely the opposite: a sacrificial rededication to her husband's interests.

One more aspect of this ritualised separation should be noted at this point. This is the emphasis placed throughout on repentance and non-repentance. When Isabella protests that 'the saints in heaven/Will knit their brows' at his vow of separation, he rejects her protest with the contemptuous

>   Let not thy love
> Make thee an unbeliever,—this my vow
> Shall never, on my soul, be satisfied
> With my repentance,— (II, i, 200–3)

Later, in assuming the blame for the separation, Isabella repeats these words almost verbatim (II, i, 260–3). Ironically, they are both speaking more truly than they realise. For Isabella will not let her love for Brachiano make her an unbeliever, either in her husband or in God. The Duke, however, has already become an unbeliever so far as Isabella is concerned, and will soon be so (he describes himself in IV, ii as 'an heathen sacrifice') in relation to God, though these changes are due rather to his present dotage on Vittoria than to Isabella's former dotage upon him. In the same way, while Isabella will never have to repent her vow (which is not a vow at all), Brachiano will never choose to repent his, and will pay for his obstinacy with his soul.

Brachiano owes Isabella a debt of gratitude: he repays it by arranging her murder with Doctor Julio. At the same time he leaves Flamineo to despatch Camillo 'by such a politic strain,/Men shall suppose him by's own engine slain'. Ironically, Camillo is himself present, talking to Francisco, Monticelso, and Marcello, while this is being decided. As Brachiano, Flamineo, and the Doctor leave, the others come forward to continue their discussion, which turns first on Camillo's cuckoldry, and the scandal it has caused. Then comes one of Webster's celebrated tales, that of the proposed marriage of Phoebus. At first sight it seems to justify all the strictures which have been directed at this aspect of the dramatist's art, though Francisco deems it applicable to Vittoria. A closer look shows, however, that it is highly apposite, and easily interpreted once we recognise that Jove is God, and that Phoebus, the sun, is to be taken both as Lucifer (hence the play on 'fireworks') and Vittoria, the white devil. Francisco's point is that it would be as calamitous for Vittoria to have children, as it would were the Devil himself to do so:

> Her issue (should not providence prevent it)
> Would make both nature, time, and man repent it. (II, i, 355–6)

For all that Francisco is confident of providential intervention, however, he and Monticelso still feel a need to participate themselves in the chastisement of Vittoria and Brachiano. Their aims are, at this stage, still limited: they wish to shame Brachiano into repentance. Yet in Monticelso's pessimistic prediction, 'Sure he'll not leave her', there is already a hint of failure, while in Francisco's reply, as harsh as it is laconic, we can sense the catastrophe to come:

> There's small pity in't—
> Like mistletoe on sere elms spent by weather,
> Let him cleave to her and both rot together. (II, i, 396–8)

The dumb shows

Gunnar Boklund, discussing what he feels to be 'remarkably old-fashioned' dramatic techniques employed by Webster in *The White Devil*, says:

> Although Webster was short of space at this juncture and the dumb-shows are in a way a suitably dream-like realisation of Vittoria's evil dream, it would be hard to argue that they represent the best solution available.[3]

[3] *The Sources of The White Devil*, p. 68.

It is true that the dumb show is, in a sense, an old-fashioned device in a play first performed in 1612. In origin medieval, it was certainly used more frequently by Elizabethan dramatists than by their Jacobean successors. Yet it would be foolish on that account to stigmatise Webster's use of it here, or to assume, with Boklund, that the dramatist is taking 'the easiest way out of a difficulty' by doing so. An examination will show, in fact, that Webster chose to present the murders of Isabella and Camillo in mime because he felt that major benefits, both dramatic and thematic, would result.

The scene opens, as Brachiano informs us, at 'dead midnight', the hour traditionally appointed for the exercise of the black arts, when the Conjurer who accompanies the Duke has promised to show him 'how the intended murder of Camillo,/And our loathed duchess grow to action' (II, i, 3–4). The Conjurer is nervous. Nevertheless, money speaks. Brachiano has paid him well, and the Conjurer prepares to risk both their necks in revealing to the Duke, in the first of the dumb shows, 'the circumstance that breaks your duchess' heart'. Once again there is ambivalence in the turn of phrase. Isabella's heart will indeed 'break' when she kisses the poisoned picture. In a sense, however, it has already been 'broken' by Brachiano's cruelty, as Isabella's parting words in II, i— 'Unkindness do thy office, poor heart break'—have indicated.

The circumstances of Isabella's death further strengthen our capacity for evaluating the incident. The Duchess is murdered while demonstrating her love for her husband. The act of devotion, which the Conjurer tells Brachiano was a daily one, is highly ritualised—she 'draws the curtain of the picture, does three reverences to it, and kisses it thrice'— and recalls the devotions performed before an altar-piece. Brachiano, on the other hand, has once more fulfilled Cornelia's prophecy, and like Judas, betrayed love with a kiss. Unmoved even by the spectacle of his son's grief, he simply expresses his satisfaction: 'Excellent, then she's dead.'

The failure of Flamineo's aim to make Camillo's death seem accidental —a 'far more politic fate'—is indicated by the fact that Francisco immediately has him and his accomplices arrested. It is not the last time we will see one of Flamineo's much-vaunted schemes fail.

Brachiano's reaction to the murder of Camillo is that of a connoisseur, appreciative, but anxious not to miss the full savour of what he has before him. The Conjurer therefore explains what the Duke has just witnessed, thereby also underlining the callous enjoyment which

Brachiano has derived from the murders. Not even the news that Francisco has ordered Vittoria's arrest, news that forces Brachiano to leave her house hurriedly, can spoil his good humour. Shaking hands with the Conjurer, he assures him of his reward:

> Noble friend,
> You bind me ever to you,—this shall stand
> As the firm seal annexed to my hand.
> It shall enforce a payment. (II, ii, 52–5)

For the Duke, it is to be a terrible payment.

THE MIDDLE

The trial

By its setting, in an ante-chamber adjoining the papal consistory, III, i prepares us for the trial of Vittoria. As a prologue should, it provides us with the terms of reference within which the action is to be conducted, bringing together the participants—except, for good dramatic reasons, Vittoria and Brachiano—and indicating briefly the manner in which they will behave during the trial.

We learn first of the aims and methods of the prosecutors, Francisco and Monticelso, witnessing their admission that they 'have naught but circumstances' to charge Vittoria with, and hearing that they nonetheless hope to 'make her infamous/To all our neighbouring kingdoms' by trying her in the presence of 'all the grave lieger ambassadors'. Their aim is still, it seems, to shame Brachiano into breaking off the liaison.

As the prosecutors leave, two of the defendants, Flamineo and Marcello, enter under guard and attended by a lawyer. At first the discussion is light-hearted, with the lawyer trying Flamineo's wit, and being exposed as 'a dull ass' for his pains. With Flamineo's admission that he has merely 'put on this feigned garb of mirth/To gull suspicion', however, the conversation takes a more serious turn, resolving itself into an argument between the two brothers over Vittoria, and thence over means and ends.

To Flamineo morality is irrelevant. His touchstone is material gain, and Vittoria's beauty is simply an asset, 'a kind of path/To her and mine own preferment'. Marcello, however, takes his stand on orthodox moral principles, and regards the path Flamineo and his sister are treading as leading to ruin rather than reward. Largely because he can point to the poor rewards Marcello has gained for risking his life as a soldier, Flamineo seems to win the argument. His victory is, however, pyrrhic, because all that he says by way of disparagement about Marcello's career applies to his own. He follows a 'great duke' and, before paying for the fact with his 'prodigal blood', will find that his reward is as elusive as a 'poor handful' of water. He will find, in short, that events prove his view of life to be 'lamented doctrine', and that for all its apparent unworldliness Marcello's advice, 'For love of virtue bear an honest heart', is a more reliable guide to living.

The impact of the ceremonial opening of the next scene with the entry of the six ambassadors in procession with Francisco, Monticelso, the lawyer, the four prisoners—Vittoria, Zanche, Flamineo, and Marcello —and a guard, is blurred by the presence of 'an unbidden guest'. Brachiano resists Monticelso's suggestion that he should leave, and with a display of nonchalance, spreads his gown to recline on. Though Monticelso handles a difficult moment well, his plans have been upset. At any moment, Brachiano may rudely disrupt the dignified proceedings of the court.

The brush with Brachiano is followed by another contretemps for the prosecution, the defeat of the Latin-speaking lawyer. The episode, which might at first be taken for no more than a moment of comic relief, is in fact essential to the success of the whole scene. In the first place, the victory enables Vittoria to establish a tactical ascendancy over her accusers. She will not finally succeed in refuting their charges, but she will defend herself with courage and élan, winning our admiration if not our approval. Secondly, the episode enables Webster to satisfy the requirements of verisimilitude while at the same time providing for the more subtle needs of symbolic truth and dramatic effect. Technically, Monticelso is Vittoria's judge, and the ambassadors constitute a kind of jury. But to have the lawyer as prosecutor would muffle the dramatic effect by interposing him between the protagonists; without him, a direct confrontation is possible, with Monticelso, stung by Vittoria's taunts, coming into the open as her accuser, and the ambassadors serving *ad hoc* as judges. Finally, Vittoria's objection to her case being heard in Latin, because 'amongst this auditory/Which come to hear my cause, the half or more/May be ignorant in't', cleverly supplies a reason for continuing the proceedings in the vernacular and gains the sympathy of the unlettered, who would comprise a majority of the play's first audience at the Red Bull.

The lawyer gone, helped on his way by Francisco's scorn, Vittoria and Monticelso confront one another directly. The Cardinal's plan is simple—to expose Vittoria as a whore:

> You see my lords what goodly fruit she seems,
> Yet like those apples travellers report
> To grow where Sodom and Gomorrah stood,
> I will but touch her and you straight shall see
> She'll fall to soot and ashes. (III, ii, 63–7)

Though Vittoria's courage and wit make his task far from easy, the Cardinal presses ahead with his attack. When she affects ignorance of the word 'whore', he provides a formal exposition of the term. The result is a verse equivalent of one of the most popular literary genres of the age, the prose 'character'. Monticelso's 'perfect character' follows the form, working in general terms: it is a description of whores as a type, rather than of an individual. Because it is both generalised and rhetorical, however, it should not be dismissed as empty oratory. On the contrary, its metaphoric implications are at every point relevant to the careers of Vittoria and her lover. The comparison with 'poison'd perfumes', for instance, should remind us of Isabella's death, and of Vittoria's complicity in it, while the reference to the barrenness of 'Cold Russian winters' recalls the emphasis placed on Vittoria's childlessness in the tale of Phoebus' marriage. There are prefigurative elements too. The association of weddings and funerals suggests the death of Brachiano on his wedding day, while the reference to 'treasuries by extortion fill'd,/And empty'd by curs'd riot' anticipates the dying Duke's ravings (V, iii, 83–6 and 106–8), and the comparison with the dead bodies of felons, 'which are begg'd at gallows', suggests the torments of the two 'friars' (V, iii, 150–4). All in all, though Vittoria claims that 'this character scapes me', we are brought to a deeper understanding of the fact that

> She's like the guilty counterfeited coin
> Which whosoe'er first stamps it brings in trouble
> All that receive it. (III, ii, 99–101)

After Monticelso's rhetoric, we need a brief space in which to pause and evaluate. This the English and French Ambassadors provide in their succinct summary of proceedings to date:

Cw

Fr. Amb.   She hath lived ill.
Eng. Amb.   True, but the cardinal's too bitter. (III, ii, 106–7)

Tacitly acknowledging the validity of this criticism, Monticelso aban-
dons vituperation, and turns from 'the devil, Adult'ry' to 'the devil,
Murder'. Joined by Francisco, he proceeds to cross-examine Vittoria
about the suspicious circumstances surrounding Camillo's death. When
they accuse her of 'cunning', she appeals to the Ambassadors, claiming
that she is forced to 'personate masculine virtue' when 'entangled in a
cursed accusation'. Once again the English Ambassador sums up the
audience reaction: 'She hath a brave spirit.' We admire her bearing, if
not her behaviour. In her lover's case, we can admire neither. Silent
throughout the onslaught on Vittoria's character, he is drawn into
proceedings only when directly implicated by Monticelso's questioning.
At first he is impudently assured, justifying his association with Vittoria
in terms of 'charity'. But then he loses his temper, and having threatened
his opponent, storms out, leaving Vittoria to face her accusers alone.

Up to this point the cross-examination has dealt mainly with Camillo's
death, and Vittoria at least has created the impression that she is on trial
for her life. Francisco's advice to the Cardinal—'The act of blood let
pass, only descend/To matter of incontinence'—reminds us that she is,
in fact, only on trial for her liberty and reputation. These Vittoria
defends vigorously, making the most of the weaknesses in her opponents'
case, and presenting herself skilfully as an example of wronged innocence.
Knowing as much as we do, however, we should by now be beginning
to see that her plausibility is her most dangerous feature, that the Cardinal is right when he says, 'If the devil/Did ever take good shape
behold his picture'.

The cross-examination over, Monticelso sums up. He aims to ad-
minister 'a choke-pear' to Vittoria by exposing her as 'a most notorious
strumpet', but the terms in which he does so—they include the idiom,
'I yet but draw the curtain—now to your picture'—remind us that she
is guilty of much graver sins than adultery. Because we are aware of
Vittoria's part in the murder of Isabella, we know she has got off very
lightly in merely being 'confin'd/Unto a house of convertites'. She may
protest that Monticelso has 'ravish'd justice', but in fact she has received
a sentence both just and merciful, considering the 'corrupted trial' she
has made of her 'life and beauty'.

Throughout the trial, Webster has induced a response to Vittoria embracing both admiration and condemnation. This balance is maintained to the end, for in her response to her sentence Vittoria first forfeits our respect with her violent outburst of curses, threats, and vituperation, then regains it with the superb (if in some respects dishonest) statement of defiance with which she concludes. Even so, the final note is not one of approbation, since the entry of Brachiano, hypocritically mourning the 'news' of Isabella's death, brings Vittoria's guilt to mind once more, while the real grief of Giovanni stresses the suffering the innocent must endure while the lovers indulge their passion.

Flamineo and Lodovico

One of the most widely used and dramatically useful of all Elizabethan and Jacobean dramatic conventions was that which assumed that in their ravings the mad reveal profound truths. Later in *The White Devil* Brachiano is to do just this. Equally valuable was the extension of this convention which required that those feigning insanity, as Flamineo does in III, iii, should do the same. The 'mad humour' which he assumes is, in fact, a device to 'keep off idle questions', but because he is at pains to make it seem a result of Vittoria's disgrace, Flamineo dwells on the perils of a parasite's career. As he does so, allowing his cynical but inventive wit full play, he makes many comments whose ironic applicability to his own circumstances will become clear as the play proceeds.

One such significant remark is his comment on the Ambassadors:

If they were rack'd now to know the confederacy! But your noblemen are privileged from the rack; (III, iii, 35–6)

The sentiment echoes that expressed in the opening moments of the play by Lodovico (I, i, 38 ff.), which still seems to be true. By the end of the play, however, Flamineo will be of a different opinion.

While Flamineo is speaking, Lodovico and Marcello are standing by. Lodovico is both curious and suspicious 'that in such open and apparent guilt/Of his adulterous sister, he dare utter/So scandalous a passion'. Flamineo is equally suspicious, wondering how Lodovico dare return from banishment without a pardon. In hopes of satisfying their suspicions, the two men begin sparring verbally. As they do so, Marcello, momentarily cast in the role of 'presenter', advises us to 'mark this strange encounter'. Strange it indeed is, yet it is also significant, for it brings the two men together for the only time in the play prior to the final catastrophe, and shows both how much they have in common— wit, cynicism, and an amoral and self-seeking attitude to the world—and how certain it is, because they are alike, that they must clash violently in pursuit of reward. The blow struck by Flamineo is a foretaste of what is to come. When Vittoria and Flamineo face their murderers in the last scene, Lodovico will be seeking revenge for himself, as well as for his master.

First moves towards revenge

The failure of their scheme to shame Brachiano into repentance forces Francisco and Monticelso to reconsider their plans, and to choose whether to take more drastic steps, or (as orthodoxy required) to leave matters in the hands of God. In II, i it seemed that, of the two, Monticelso was the more thirsty for vengeance. The first thirty lines of IV, i seem to confirm this view, for when Francisco disclaims all thoughts of revenge, the Cardinal rebukes him for being 'turn'd all marble', and counters the Duke's fear of involving his subjects in a war with Brachiano with a counsel of Machiavellian patience:

> Bear your wrongs conceal'd,
> And, patient as the tortoise, let this camel
> Stalk o'er your back unbruis'd: sleep with the lion,
> And let this brood of secure foolish mice
> Play with your nostrils, till the time be ripe
> For th'bloody audit, and the fatal gripe: (IV, i, 14–19)

Though the ostentation of Ferdinand's disclaimers ought to have made us suspicious, it is not until he has an opportunity to comment in soliloquy (IV, i, 37–42) that we become aware of the extent of his double-dealing, or of the reasons for his circumspection. The Duke's suspicion that the Cardinal is not as vengeful as he professes to be leads us to be equally careful in evaluating Monticelso's words, and to wonder whether he was not perhaps encouraging Francisco to 'untie' his 'folded thoughts' in order to be able to counter any scheme for revenge. At this stage we cannot tell: the ambiguity which surrounds the Cardinal's character and motives will not be resolved until IV, iii.

About Francisco, however, there can no longer be any doubt. Having borrowed from the Cardinal that catalogue of 'the names of all notorious offenders/Lurking about the city', his 'black book' where 'lurk/The names of many devils', he proceeds to search it for 'a list of murderers,/ Agents for any villainy'. From it he selects Lodovico as the man most capable of carrying out his plans. That Brachiano is to be murdered is clear. That Francisco is willing to go to any lengths to achieve revenge is also clear from the line from the *Aeneid* with which the scene concludes: '*Flectere si nequeo superos, Acheronta movebo*'—'If I cannot prevail upon the gods above, I will move the regions of Acheron.' Having failed to obtain justice, Francisco is to abandon the path of orthodoxy, and seek aid from Hell.

One aspect of IV, i remains undiscussed: the appearance of Isabella's ghost. From the first, the supernatural formed an accepted part of revenge tragedy. Its function, however, varied. In Kyd's *Spanish Tragedy*, for instance, the ghost of Don Andrea takes no part in the action, but joins the figure of Revenge in providing a comment on the play's action. In *Hamlet*, on the other hand, the ghost of the dead king participates in the action, guiding and encouraging the hero in the prosecution of revenge. The part played by the ghosts in *The White Devil* (Isabella's here and Brachiano's in V, iv) resembles these less, however, than it does the role of Banquo's ghost in *Macbeth*. Like Banquo's ghost, they say nothing, and may be taken as figments of the viewer's imagination, since no one else sees them. In *Macbeth* Shakespeare leaves this question open, making it possible for his audience either to accept one of the traditional beliefs concerning ghosts—that they were the spirits of those in purgatory (a view discredited by Protestant disbelief in the existence of such a state), or were angels or devils which had assumed the forms of the dead for their own purposes, good or bad—or to follow the sceptic, Reginald Scot, in taking them to be illusions engendered by an excess of melancholy.[4] Webster, interestingly, stresses Francisco's belief in Scot's theory:

> Let me remember my dead sister's face:
> Call for her picture: no; I'll close mine eyes,
> And in a melancholic thought I'll frame
> Her figure 'fore me. (IV, i, 99–102)

And again, when Isabella appears:

[4] See J. Dover Wilson, *What Happens in Hamlet* (Cambridge, 1967), pp. 60–6.

> Thought, as a subtle juggler, makes us deem
> Things supernatural, which have cause
> Common as sickness. 'Tis my melancholy, (IV, i, 107–9)

Francisco's view is not necessarily Webster's, of course, and we may wonder whether we are meant, in fact, to disapprove of the Duke's scepticism, and see the ghost as a devil in human form. The question is never resolved.

The lovers' quarrel

It is tempting, from time to time, to compare Vittoria and Brachiano with those archetypes of a total commitment to love, Antony and Cleopatra. For the most part, such comparisons are pointless, whether made in terms of character or theme. In one direction, however, a valid comparison can be made. We judge the validity of Antony's rejection of the world of political and military glory according to our assessment of the quality of his relationship with Cleopatra. Their love being what it is, the world is well lost. If we ask the same question about Brachiano's choice, we are forced to conclude that his rejection of 'dukedom, health, wife, children, friends and all' is a disastrous mistake, not simply because he damns himself in the process, but also because the quality of their love is inadequate. In IV, ii this fact is brought very forcefully to our attention as the lovers quarrel.

It is not the mere fact that a quarrel occurs which is so significant, but the ease with which Francisco engineers a rift between Vittoria and Brachiano, and the deep distrust and antagonism which the quarrel exposes. Though with the help of Flamineo the lovers are eventually reconciled, and though, indeed, we can still believe, at the end of the scene, in the passionate intensity of the bond which unites them, the suspicion and jealousy which their bitter accusations and counter-accusations have brought to the surface have diminished in our eyes both them and their love.

The scene opens with the Matron of the House of Convertites nervously complaining to Flamineo about Brachiano's visits to Vittoria. The note of furtiveness which her speech introduces is soon drowned out by the anger which Francisco's letter to Vittoria arouses. The Duke's plan succeeds perfectly: the servant delivers the letter to the Matron with ostentatious secrecy, and Brachiano, suspicious, seizes and opens it. The discovery that it is from Francisco enrages him: its contents, carefully contrived to arouse his jealousy, incense him further. On the audience, however, one part of the letter has a different effect. Insinuating that Brachiano has deserted her, Francisco compares Vittoria's plight with that of a vine whose 'prop is fall'n'. Recalling as it does the earlier image of Vittoria as a vine manured with blood (III, ii, 184–8), it reminds us, unobtrusively, that her fate is not undeserved.

Brachiano's response to the letter is as unreflective and intemperate as Francisco could have wished: without stopping to consider the possibility of a trick, he brands Vittoria a whore and diseased. Flamineo's reaction is equally violent, partly, it seems, out of a vestigial sense of family honour, and partly out of a fear that his hopes of advancement are in jeopardy. Unable to out-threaten his secretary, Brachiano tries to assert his authority with 'Do you know me?' In Flamineo's reply we find not only an ironic and self-deprecatory awareness of the insecurity of the parasite's world, but also a choric expression of the play's deeper meaning:

> O my lord! methodically.
> As in this world there are degrees of evils:
> So in this world there are degrees of devils.
> You're a great duke; I your poor secretary. (IV, ii, 57–60)

Abusing Vittoria without explaining why, Brachiano is quick to repudiate any responsibility for the past:

> Your beauty! O, ten thousand curses on't.
> How long have I beheld the devil in crystal?
> Thou hast led me, like an heathen sacrifice,
> With music, and with fatal yokes of flowers
> To my eternal ruin. (IV, ii, 87–91)

Equally quickly, he experiences a revulsion of feeling in favour of Isabella, but Vittoria prevents him from indulging in maudlin self-pity by recalling his part in his wife's death. Then she draws his attention to her own situation, to the fact that she is 'shunn'd/By those of choicer nostrils', and to the 'incontinent college' to which he has had 'the honour to advance Vittoria'. Unlike her lover, she makes no attempt to shrug off responsibility for what she has done; rather she admits her sins and vows repentance:

> I had a limb corrupted to an ulcer,
> But I have cut it off: and now I'll go
> Weeping to heaven on crutches. (IV, ii, 121–3)

One cannot, of course, be sure that in saying this Vittoria is not simply seeking to outmanœuvre Brachiano. Whether this is so or not, however, her behaviour is more admirable than the mixture of bluster and evasion characteristic of the Duke throughout the scene.

While the lovers' quarrel was at its height, Flamineo prudently stood aside. When, however, Brachiano tries to regain favour with Vittoria, Flamineo is quick to intercede. As he does so, alternately encouraging the Duke and pleading with Vittoria, he provides us again with a debased and cynical commentary on the lovers and their relationship. Vittoria's will is compared to 'a damn'd imposthume', or abcess, and she herself to shop-soiled goods. She is a tortoise or a levret, while Brachiano is the timorous ferret, ready to relinquish his hold on Vittoria at the slightest sign of resistance. Increasingly, such comments come between us and the lovers, preventing us from according their grand passion romantic approval by ensuring that we are aware of its base and criminal aspects.

Three examples of this are particularly worthy of note. One is Flamineo's comment, 'Mark his penitence'. This is meant to placate Vittoria, but it also serves another end, recalling the occasion when Brachiano vowed never to repent of his 'divorce' from Isabella, and providing a link in the chain of cause and effect which will end on the Duke's death-bed. There is a similar relevance in Flamineo's serio-comic comment on his master's success in subduing Vittoria: 'O we curl'd-hair'd men/Are still most kind to women'. Recalling Brachiano's treatment of Isabella and Flamineo's of his mother, we may find this ironic. The third comment carries implications of a different sort. As the couple silently embrace, the gratified pander remarks:

> I sweat for you.
> Couple together with as deep a silence
> As did the Grecians in their wooden horse. (IV, ii, 198–200)

The insinuation of homosexuality here is gratuitous, although in it is reflected something of the unsavouriness of the lovers' relationship, furtive and illicit. The reference to the wooden horse also recalls the plotting of Francisco. As gullible as the Trojans, Brachiano falls for his enemy's ruse, and adopts the plan prepared by Francisco as his own. In doing so, he is ensuring his own destruction.

The scene concludes with another of Webster's celebrated tales. Told by Flamineo, it recounts the fable, recorded by Herodotus and Pliny, of the ungrateful crocodile. Brachiano takes the crocodile to be himself, and the moral that he has insufficiently rewarded his secretary, and though Flamineo denies this, saying that it is a warning to Vittoria against ingratitude, it seems clear that the Duke is right. Though a crisis has been surmounted, and all seems to be going well, Flamineo still cannot feel secure: it is all the more ironic, therefore, that he confides to us, in an aside, that 'Knaves do grow great by being great men's apes'.

The papal election

The papal election with which IV, iii opens has been condemned as 'a touch of brilliant pageantry and dramatically inconsequential splendour being added where it serves an immediate purpose'.[5] In fact the scene is one of the most important in the play, and the elements of pageantry it includes serve a serious purpose, closely linked to the play's deepest thematic preoccupations. The almost antiquarian care with which Webster describes the method of election, the emphasis he places on the means by which secrecy is assured and coercion prevented, the presence of the ambassadors in their robes of chivalry as a sign of the dignity of the occasion—all these are designed to convince us that Monticelso's candidacy has been honest and in strict accordance with canon law, not like that of the Cardinal in *The Duchess of Malfi* who, in seeking the papal throne, 'did bestow bribes, so largely, and so impudently, as if he would have carried it away without heavens knowledge' (I, i, 165-6). Webster's departure from history in making Monticelso choose the title of Paul IV is yet another measure designed to put the moral standing of the new pope beyond question. Had the dramatist followed history in naming him Sixtus V, the new pope would immediately have been suspect as the pontiff who had preached rebellion against Queen Elizabeth and encouraged Spanish plans for the invasion of Britain.

Monticelso's election, honestly though it has been carried out, cannot at once free him from suspicion. We need to know much more before we can feel sure that Francisco is right in assuming that the Cardinal has abandoned all thought of revenge. Playing on this uncertainty, Webster is able to achieve considerable dramatic tension. The news of Vittoria's flight from Rome, following hard on the announcement of Monticelso's election, arouses our expectation that he will act decisively

5 Boklund, *The Sources of The White Devil*, p. 68.

against her and her lover. We must first, however, observe Francisco's reaction to the news, a reaction which bears further witness to his cunning. He rejoices in secret at the success of his scheming, seeing it as a prelude to more violent action:

> Thy fame, fond duke,
> I first have poison'd; directed thee the way
> To marry a whore; what can be worse? This follows:
> The hand must act to drown the passionate tongue,—
> I scorn to wear a sword and prate of wrong. (IV, iii, 54–8)

After Francisco's threats comes Christian forgiveness in the form of the papal blessing and absolution pronounced by Monticelso. The juxtaposition highlights the significance of the choice Vittoria and Brachiano made in the previous scene. Had they accepted the decision of the papal court in the hopes of an eventual pardon for Vittoria, they would not have put themselves in the hands of their enemies. The Pope's response to the news of their flight is limited to a formal statement of excommunication. This is sufficient, however, to put them outside the jurisdiction or protection of the Church, thus making the way clear for Francisco.

By juxtaposing Francisco's lust for revenge and Monticelso's restraint, and by continuing to contrast the behaviour of the two men, arranging their exits and entrances so that for the remainder of IV, iii they appear alternately in conversation with Lodovico, Webster brings us to see that their divergent views are only a sign of a more serious and fundamental divergence. Which course is Francisco's is underlined by his opening question to Lodovico:

> Come dear Lodovico,
> You have ta'en the sacrament to prosecute
> Th'intended murder. (IV, iii, 71–3)

This perversion of religion recurs in the question Monticelso puts to Lodovico later about his association with Francisco:

> I know you're cunning. Come, what devil was that
> That you were raising?
> *Lod.*   Devil, my lord?
> *Mont.*   I ask you
> How doth the duke employ you, that his bonnet
> Fell with such compliment unto his knee
> When he departed from you? (IV, iii, 88–92)

When, after some prevarication, Lodovico agrees to divulge what he and Francisco intend, he provides against a possible breach of faith on Monticelso's part by announcing that he speaks not 'as an intelligencer/ But as a penitent sinner', and reminding the pontiff of the secrecy of the confessional. Inasmuch as he cannot tell others what he has learned, and is thus prevented from organising counter-measures, Monticelso is indeed 'o'erta'en'. As a confessor, however, he has both the opportunity and the obligation to advise the penitent. This he does in a speech which, particularly in its reference to the yew, implies a direct link between the revengers' guilt and that of their intended victims:

> Dost thou imagine thou canst slide on blood
> And not be tainted with a shameful fall?
> Or like the black, and melancholic yew tree,
> Dost think to root thyself in dead men's graves,
> And yet to prosper? Instruction to thee
> Comes like sweet showers to over-hard'ned ground:
> They wet, but pierce not deep. And so I leave thee
> With all the Furies hanging 'bout thy neck,
> Till by thy penitence thou remove this evil,
> In conjuring from thy breast that cruel devil. (IV, iii, 118–27)

Lodovico's decision to abandon his plan of revenge is largely due to the vehemence of Monticelso's denunciation, but the new Pope's forbearance also influences him:

> I'll give it o'er. He says 'tis damnable:
> Besides I did expect his suffrage,
> By reason of Camillo's death. (IV, iii, 128–30)

At the last, Monticelso's moral standing has been put beyond doubt. Convincing the sinner both by his teaching and his example, the new Pope has proved himself a true pastor.

Having come to confession in mockery, Lodovico leaves it genuinely penitent. He is not, however, long to be allowed to remain so. Encountering temptation as he leaves the confessional, he falls into sin once more. The tempter is Francisco; his bait, gold. The success of his scheme, however, is assured by his exploitation of Lodovico's cynicism. Regarding himself as 'doubly arm'd' for revenge, Lodovico generalises about the evils of great men:

> There's but three Furies found in spacious hell,
> But in a great man's breast three thousand dwell. (IV, iii, 152–3)

It is his tragedy to apply this couplet, so accurate as a general assessment of the great in the world of *The White Devil*, to Monticelso, the one great man who does not deserve it.

THE END

Flamineo's fall

Were *The White Devil* to be interpreted in terms of the traditional tragic concept of fortune's wheel (and we may wonder whether an orthodox *de casibus* schema may not underlie the action), the first scene of Act V would be found to represent that moment when, having seemingly overcome all opposition, the aspirant stands triumphant at the top of the wheel, unaware that the inevitable descent into misery and death is about to commence. Vittoria and Brachiano are married, and Flamineo feels secure:

> In all the weary minutes of my life,
> Day ne'er broke up till now. This marriage
> Confirms me happy. (V, i, 1–3)

Though Hortensio may agree with Flamineo that the marriage is 'a good assurance', he unwittingly draws attention, however, to the threat which (as yet unperceived) hangs over the lovers and their parasite. Ironically, it is Flamineo, who so prides himself on his clear-sightedness, who furnishes us with an enthusiastic account of 'the Moor that's come to court', and of the 'two noblemen of Hungary' who accompany him. Even more ironic, in the light of subsequent events, is the emphasis placed on the fact that all three are dedicated Christians. The 'Hungarians', for instance, are described as having

> ent'red into religion, into the strict order of Capuchins: but being
> not well settled in their undertaking they left their order and returned
> to court: for which being after troubled in conscience, they vowed
> their service against the enemies of Christ; (V, i, 15–19)

When, later, our suspicions about the identity of Mulinassar are confirmed, we will come to appreciate the aptness of their disguise as

Capuchins. Later still, in V, iii, the behaviour of the 'friars' at the bedside of Brachiano will show the resilience of their consciences, even in the service of the enemies of Christ.

During his brief, ceremonial appearance in V, i, Brachiano makes it plain that he shares his secretary's golden opinion of the new arrivals. How fatally misguided is this enthusiasm is made clear once Mulinassar and the friars are alone with Carlo and Pedro, two of those members of Brachiano's court to whom Francisco had, in IV, iii, referred as being his 'faction' and 'counsel'.[6] As the six men confer, they recall the sacrilegious impression made earlier by Francisco and Lodovico, when Carlo proclaims that he and Pedro have 'our vows seal'd with the sacrament/To second your attempts', and when Lodovico voices his regret at being unable to kill Brachiano in a way which would ensure the destruction of soul as well as body. In the event, Brachiano dies in a manner which indicates unmistakably despair and damnation, after inviting his end so completely that, as Pedro says, 'He could not have invented his own ruin,/Had he despair'd, with more propriety'.

A similarly irreligious element is noticeable, too, in the conversation between Flamineo, Marcello, and Zanche, whose entry forces the conspirators to disperse. 'Why doth this devil haunt you?' Marcello demands, angry at Flamineo's association with Zanche. 'I know not,' replies Flamineo, affecting carelessness,

> For by this light I do not conjure for her.
> 'Tis not so great a cunning as men think
> To raise the devil: for here's one up already,—
> The greatest cunning were to lay him down— (V, i, 86–90)

At first sight no more than a slighting reference to Zanche's persistence, the exchange in fact provides the key to her role in the play, and the reason why Webster substituted a Moor for the Greek waiting-woman of the historical narrative. Paralleling in her relationship with Flamineo her mistress's liaison with Brachiano, Zanche is the black devil to Vittoria's white. Recognising this, we can find a wealth of significance in Zanche's attraction to her 'countryman', Mulinassar. Her announcement that she intends to 'discourse with him/In our own language' has been criticised as a red herring, falsely leading us to assume that

---

[6] Brown, Revels *White Devil*, p. 126 n., convincingly disposes of the generally held view that Carlo and Pedro are merely Lodovico and Gasparo in disguise.

when Zanche does this, Francisco will be exposed. In fact it is intended to underline their kinship, to stress the rightness, in symbolic terms, of the Duke's black disguise.

The departure of Zanche is followed by a discussion between Flamineo, Marcello and Francisco which, for all its seemingly random course, touches on three of the play's major preoccupations: the illusory nature of greatness, courtly reward and punishment, and the partiality of earthly justice. The terms in which Francisco discourses on the subject of justice are particularly interesting:

> you shall see in the country in harvest time, pigeons, though they destroy never so much corn, the farmer dare not present the fowling piece to them! why? because they belong to the lord of the manor; whilst your poor sparrows that belong to the lord of heaven, they go to the pot for't. (V, i, 127–32)

His complaint, it will be seen, is essentially that voiced by Lodovico in I, i and Flamineo in III, i. What is new is the implied disparity between human and divine justice. On this point increasing emphasis will be laid.

With the departure of Francisco and the return of Zanche, accompanied by Hortensio, 'the morality of your sunburnt gentleman' (as Flamineo puts it) gives way to a discussion of love. Amid the banter, however, serious undertones can be detected. When, for instance, Hortensio asks his opinion of 'perfum'd gallants', Flamineo replies:

> Their satin cannot save them. I am confident
> They have a certain spice of the disease,
> For they that sleep with dogs, shall rise with fleas. (V, i, 165–8)

The pun on 'satin' and 'satan', and the reference to dogs, which follows hard on Flamineo's description of himself as 'a frighted dog with a bottle at's tail', are comments on his own fate: his witticism affirms the inevitability of a retribution which not even those in the service of the Devil can evade.

The timing of the remark is apt, for within minutes Flamineo has, by quarrelling with Marcello, begun the descent which leaves him, at the end of V, ii, a convicted murderer, helpless in the hands of an employer who will neither forgive nor forget that his secretary once defied him (V, ii, 72–6).

Of the deeper significance of his brother's death, Flamineo seems at this stage entirely unaware: the murder is simply a 'misfortune', its effect on his career more important than the death itself. What Flamineo fails to comprehend is made plain to us, however, through the comments of Cornelia and Marcello. The latter's concern is with causes: to him the incident is evidence of divine disapproval of Flamineo's and Vittoria's efforts 'to rise/By all dishonest means'. Cornelia, on the other hand, thinks rather of Flamineo's need to 'spend the time to come/In blest repentance'. Juding by his indifference to Marcello's death, he will not heed her.

The death of Brachiano

Having shown Flamineo's abrupt fall from happiness and security to the miseries of a life held only on a daily lease, Webster goes on to demonstrate the even more catastrophic decline in Brachiano's fortunes, which takes him within one scene from the exercise of total power to an ignominious death. In the last moments of V, ii, just as Flamineo is submitting to Brachiano's authority, Lodovico sprinkles the Duke's helmet with poison. This act confers bitterly ironic overtones on Flamineo's comment, 'Your will is law now, I'll not meddle with it'. Both in matter and in manner, this episode is a foretaste of what is to come. Throughout V, iii, we will find the same situation, with the Duke helpless in the hands of an adversary more cunning and better prepared than himself, giving rise to the same ironies, in part perceived by the participants, in part not, and directed towards the same end. As with Flamineo, so with Brachiano we are not merely to observe the catastrophe, but also to be reminded of causes and made aware of effects.

From the first, verbal echoes and parallels are used to point up the reasons for Brachiano's death. Vittoria's cry, 'O my loved lord,—poisoned?', for instance, echoes in part the rejected Isabella's cry at II, i, 159, while Giovanni's lament reminds us of the 'sorrow express'd in Giovanni' prescribed in the dumb show. More emphatically, Brachiano's order that his son be taken away, and his warning to Vittoria, 'Do not kiss me, for I shall poison thee', enforce a recollection of the kiss that brought about Isabella's death, and of Giovanni's complaint that 'They wrapp'd her in a cruel fold of lead,/And would not let me kiss her'. In the same connection, we may note the irony of the Duke's attack on his physician as a 'most corrupted politic hangman', one able to 'kill without book', but lacking the 'art to save'. In II, i, by contrast, he had addressed Doctor Julio as 'honest doctor' when asking him to exercise his 'skill' as a poisoner.

Now the groundwork is laid for another stage in the retributive process. 'This unction is sent from the great Duke of Florence', says Brachiano. To which Mulinassar gravely replies,' Sir be of comfort.' The provision of spiritual comfort and the administration of extreme unction being the duties of the priest towards the dying, it is appropriate that Francisco's followers, the 'Hungarian friars', should now enter. 'What are those?' asks Brachiano. 'Franciscans,' replies Flamineo, underlining an irony previously available only to those who were aware that the Capuchins were an offshoot of the Franciscan order, 'They have brought the extreme unction.'

At this point we expect to see the two 'friars' exercise their 'priestly office'. Instead Brachiano withdraws to an inner room. Though it might seem to constitute a break in continuity, this withdrawal serves valuable dramatic and thematic purposes. First, it takes the focus off the Duke until the climax of his suffering is reached, ensuring thereby that his insanity has the maximum impact. Second, it provides time for a discussion by Flamineo and Francisco which, in emphasising 'what solitariness is about dying princes', recalls Cornelia's prophecy in I, ii. Lastly, it enables the nature and significance of Brachiano's ravings to be explained before we observe them. 'His mind fastens/On twenty several objects, which confound/Deep sense with folly,' Lodovico says. The truth of his observations is shown by the first speech Brachiano makes upon his return, 'presented in a bed', as the Quarto directs. Vittoria cannot have illegally exported coin, and is unlikely to have 'bought and sold offices'. But she does need to make up her accounts, just as Brachiano himself does, as his dying visions make clear. First he sees the devil 'in a blue bonnet, and a pair of breeches/With a great codpiece'. Later 'six gray rats that have lost their tails,/Crawl up the pillow'—almost certainly witches. The inference seems obvious: Brachiano is damned.

Like the thief on the cross, however, a man may repent and be saved on his death-bed. When, therefore, Brachiano fixes his gaze so steadfastly on the crucifix that, as Vittoria says, 'It settles his wild spirits; and so his eyes/Melt into tears', we feel there is some hope for him, even though the 'Capuchin' holding the crucifix is Lodovico. Momentarily, the words of the friars seem to reinforce that hope. Then the bitter irony of the Latin phrases (florrowed, significantly enough, from the account in Erasmus' Colloquy, *Funus*, of the death of Georgius Balearicus, who 'trusting to his wealth, sought by purchase to retain his standing beyond the grave') comes to the fore. '*Esto securus Domine Brachiane*', intones Gasparo, '*cogita quantum habeas meritorum—denique memineris meam animam pro tua oppignoratam si quid esset periculi*'—Rest assured, Lord Brachiano: think how many good deeds you have done—lastly, remember that my soul is pledged for yours if there should be any peril.'

That their purpose is to induce despair (and hence, since the desperate lose all hope of God's mercy, damnation) Lodovico and Gasparo prove when, alone with the dying man, they reveal their thoughts as well as their identities. In their antiphonal duologue, they stress the fate which awaits Brachiano:

Gasp.   Brachiano.
Lod. Devil Brachiano. Thou art damn'd.
Gasp.   Perpetually.
Lod. A slave condemn'd, and given up to the gallows ,
     Is thy great lord and master.
Gasp.   True: for thou
     Art given up to the devil. (V, iii, 150–4)

In their enjoyment, Lodovico and Gasparo seek to prolong the torment first by cataloguing the poisons eating into the Duke's brain, and then (here providing yet another reminder of Cornelia's prophecy) by assuring him that he will be forgotten before his funeral sermon. At this point, however, their pleasures are interrupted by Brachiano's last great cry, 'Vittoria? Vittoria!' She enters, but is hustled out of the room again (ironically with an appeal to 'Christian charity' which echoes Brachiano's impudent use of the phrase during Vittoria's trial) and the Duke strangled with 'a true-love knot/Sent from the Duke of Florence'. 'Rest to his soul' is the courtiers' orthodox response to the news of his death. Vittoria is nearer the truth, however, when she cries, 'O me! this place is hell.' We remember Mephostophilis' reply to Faustus' question about the location of hell:

Hell hath no limits, nor is circumscrib'd
In one self place, but where we are is hell,
And where hell is, there must we ever be; (V, 122–4)

Flamineo's rather one-sided conversation with Francisco serves to relieve tension after the horrors of the death-bed, but it is not an anodyne.

Dw

On the contrary, it forces us to reconsider what we have witnessed. Debased and cynical though they are, Flamineo's comments on 'women's tears', the 'misery of princes', 'court promises' and 'court-honesty' recall to mind the thematic strands of which they are part.

The intrigue with which V, iii concludes performs much the same function. For we need not only to know what Francisco and Lodovico intend, but also to recall what has preceded it, to be reminded that the fate planned for Vittoria, Zanche, and Flamineo is not undeserved. In achieving this simultaneity of past, present, and future, Webster relies on an irony established even in the opening lines:

> *Fran.* You're passionately met in this sad world.
> *Zan.*   I would have you look up, sir; these court tears
>   Claim not your tribute to them. Let those weep
>   That guiltily partake in the sad cause. (V, iii, 219–22)

There is irony, too, in the way Zanche uses the fiction of a dream to reveal her desires, since the result of her 'dreaming' will be death, not only for herself, but also for one who had earlier used the same device to convey her wishes. Her use of terms such as 'confess' and 'contrition' both reminds us of Brachiano's carefree use of such words and loads with a double irony her hope that the hundred thousand crowns she intends stealing will constitute 'a dowry' able to 'make that sunburnt proverb false,/And wash the Ethiop white'.

In this connection we should also note the brief exchange with which the scene concludes, an exchange which not only proves that Lodovico is still troubled by the claims of morality, but also shows how far Mulinassar the Moor has travelled from the family virtues of the Duke of Florence:

> *Lod.* Why now our action's justified,—
> *Fran.*   Tush for justice.
>   What harms it justice? we now, like the partridge
>   Purge the disease with laurell: for the fame
>   Shall crown the enterprize and quit the shame. (V, iii, 267–70)

The mad scene

Because Webster clearly had Shakespeare's Ophelia in mind when writing the central section of V, iv, it is often dismissed as palely derivative. Such a view involves a failure to recognise that the focus of attention in the scene is not Cornelia, but Flamineo; that Cornelia's madness is significant chiefly in its effect upon her son.

The Flamineo of the first few lines of V, iv, witty and cynical, gives the impression of being as self-assured as ever. That the events of the previous scenes have affected him emerges first in his inept attempt to curry favour with Giovanni. His efforts meet only with the curt injunction:

> Study your prayers, sir, and be penitent,—
> 'Twere fit you'd think on what hath former bin,—
> I have heard grief nam'd the eldest child of sin. (V, iv, 21-3)

Threatened 'divinely' (and the pun is an apt one), Flamineo admits that he is 'falling to pieces already'. This feeling intensifies with the news that he is banished from the young Duke's presence, and prompts him to respond to Francisco's opening remark, 'I met even now the most piteous sight', with 'Thou met'st another here—a pitiful/Degraded courtier.'

Upon this overriding self-concern, Francisco's account of Cornelia's suffering fails to make any impression. Flamineo's decision to watch the women winding Marcello's corpse owes nothing to sympathy: it is simple curiosity, a desire to observe 'their superstitious howling.' In the face of his mother's distress, however, Flamineo finds himself unable to maintain the callousness with which he has pursued reward. His first, oblique admission of uneasiness, 'I would I were from hence', comes with her examination of his hand for the traditional marks of guilt. With the dirge it increases, and after his mother's departure he tells Francisco:

> I have a strange thing in me, to th'which
> I cannot give a name, without it be
> Compassion,— (V, iv, 113-15)

Then, in soliloquy, he reveals his feelings more fully:

> I have liv'd
> Riotously ill, like some that live in court;
> And sometimes, when my face was full of smiles
> Have felt the maze of conscience in my breast.
> Oft gay and honour'd robes those tortures try,—
> We think cag'd birds sing, when indeed they cry. (V, iv, 116-23)

Flamineo's admission alters our response to him, making it at once more complex and more sympathetic. Yet we are not led to expect any serious attempt to escape the cage which still holds him.

With the appearance of Brachiano's ghost the scene reaches its climax. He enters, so the stage direction informs us, clad 'in his leather cassock and breeches, boots, [and] a cowl', and carrying 'a pot of lily flowers with a skull in't'. The cassock (a military, not an ecclesiastical vestment) was standard attire for a stage ghost. The lilies and the skull in a pot are emblematic: the lilies a symbol of youth and beauty, the earth and the skull of death and corruption.

After Brachiano's death, Flamineo announced that he intended to 'get to th' speech of him, though forty devils/Wait on him in his livery of flames' (V, iii 209–10). The questions he puts to the ghost explain why:

> In what place art thou? in yon starry gallery,
> Or in the cursed dungeon? No? not speak?
> Pray, sir, resolve me, what religion's best
> For a man to die in? or is it in your knowledge
> To answer me how long I have to live? (V, iv, 127–31)

Receiving no answer to his last 'most necessary question' Flamineo ventures a jest. In response 'the Ghost throws earth upon him and shows him the skull'. The horror with which Flamineo reacts to this *memento mori* recalls that occasion when at Brachiano's bedside he reacted equally superstitiously to the dying man's repetition of his name:

> I do not like that he names me so often,
> Especially on's death-bed: 'tis a sign
> I shall not live long: (V, iii, 127–9)

With the departure of the ghost Flamineo tries to come to terms with what has happened. The fact that the skull and earth vanish convinces him that 'this is beyond melancholy'. He means by this that what he has witnessed is more than a figment of a disordered imagination, but we may find a second, deeper meaning appropriate. For 'beyond melancholy', according to Jacobean theories of psychology, lay despair, and it is the voice of a desperate man that we hear in the final lines:

I do dare my fate
To do its worst. Now to my sister's lodging,
And sum up all these horrors: (V, iv, 144-6)

A false step

In a dramatist less meticulous than Webster the accidental discovery
of the revengers' plans by a minor courtier might be taken as an example
of lazy or careless writing, an *ad hoc* solution to a problem raised by
dramatically unsuitable source-material. In fact every aspect of the
short scene (V, v) in which the discovery takes place has been carefully
prepared for in such a way that what seems accidental is shown to have
a kind of inevitability within the play's retributive scheme.

Again, Webster works through verbal parallels, relating statements
in V, v to antecedents in IV, iii. Thus Lodovico's objection to Francisco's
further participation in the revenge echoes his more tentative statement
on the subject at IV, iii, 74-5, while Francisco's reply carries similar
echoes. Similarly, Hortensio's comment, 'These strong court factions
that do brook no checks,/In the career oft break the riders' necks'
(V, v, 14-15), bears more than a casual relationship to the warning,
'Take you heed:/Lest the jade break your neck', which Monticelso
gives Lodovico when the latter tries to avoid revealing the plan for
revenge by inventing a story about 'a resty Barbary horse' (IV, iii, 92-8).

This last parallel, with its emphasis on the consequences of crime,
is reinforced by similarities in situation. Both Monticelso and Hortensio
become suspicious upon observing Lodovico and Francisco in conversation. Both discover what is planned, and both try to prevent the plots
from being put into effect. There is a significant difference, however,
in the action the two men take. Monticelso tries to save Lodovico from
hell, and only fails because of Francisco's cunning. Hortensio, on the
other hand, hastens to 'raise some force' in order to frustrate the murderers and bring them to book.

And here, in the distance between penitence and punishment, lies
the reason for the echoes and parallels upon which V, v is constructed.
In stressing first the similarities and then the differences between
this scene and IV, iii, Webster is able to emphasise the changed circumstances in which Francisco and Lodovico now stand. Before the murder
of Brachiano they could have drawn back in safety. Now they cannot.
As Lodovico says, entirely unaware that his words are as applicable to
himself as to Francisco:

My lord upon my soul you shall no further:
You have most ridiculously engag'd yourself
Too far already. (V, v, 1–3)

Flamineo's mock death

The sight of Vittoria at her prayers reminds us with something of a
shock how little we know about her. Is she genuinely engaged in
her devotions, or is this merely a pious façade? Or, again, is she melan-
cholic, since on the Jacobean stage the reading of a book was commonly
used as a sign of melancholia? The enigma remains.

We do know, however, the state of mind that Flamineo is in. He
comes ' 'bout worldly business', drunk, as he says, 'with wormwood
water'. Clearly he is still in that state 'beyond melancholy' into which
he sank in V, iv. Seeking reward for his services, he soon tastes further
bitterness, for the legacy Vittoria assigns him is 'that portion . . . and
no other,/Which Cain groan'd under having slain his brother'. Since
Cain was traditionally regarded as one of the two great archetypes of
despair, as well as the first fratricide and outcast, the gift is doubly
apt.[7] In the same way his rejection of Vittoria's 'bounty' is bitterly
ironic. For his failure to acquire anything more tangible than 'a most
courtly patent to beg by' increases his despair; in a sense, that is, Vittoria's
gift must be accepted even as it is refused. This irony gives rise to
another. To explain his determination to kill Vittoria and Zanche as
well as himself, Flamineo feigns a suicidal melancholia, backing it up
with a fictitious vow to Brachiano. Yet in dissembling, he is telling
the truth. He no more intends committing suicide than he does letting
Vittoria and Zanche murder him, but he *is* 'desperate', as Zanche says,
and suicide is the traditional end of despair. In acting a part, therefore,
Flamineo is revealing the truth about the state of his soul.

The irony inherent in this coalescence of pretence and reality is
heightened by Vittoria's condemnation of suicide:

> Are you grown an atheist? will you turn your body,
> Which is the goodly palace of the soul
> To the soul's slaughterhouse? O the cursed devil
> Which doth present us with all other sins

[7] On the religious significance of despair, see Arieh Sachs, 'The Religious
Despair of Dr Faustus', *Journal of English and Germanic Philology*, LXIII
(1964), 625–47. It is interesting to note, in view of the parallels between
Flamineo's 'death' and Brachiano's, and of the Duke's 'Judas-like' behaviour, that the other great archetype of despair was Judas Iscariot.

Thrice candied o'er; despair with gall and stibium,
Yet we carouse it off;— [aside] cry out for help, —
Makes us forsake that which was made for man,
The world, to sink to that was made for devils,
Eternal darkness. (V, vi, 56–64)

Flamineo, naturally enough, rejects her argument as spurious. In one
sense, of course, he is right, as the aside to Zanche proves. In another,
however, he is wrong, for in terms of orthodox moral theology Vittoria's
argument is not mere pulpit oratory, but both reasonable and 'sound
doctrine'.

Unable to dissuade Flamineo from his 'vow' to Brachiano, Vittoria
and Zanche seek to trick him into dying first. To this end they adopt a
stoic pose akin to that which Flamineo has already taken up. This
double bluff has a comic potential which Webster exploits to the full,
but also an underlying seriousness. Zanche's emulation of her mistress's
vow to sacrifice her life for her lover, for instance, reminds us that
Webster is presenting the two relationships in parallel, while Vittoria's
fear that a botched suicide attempt might bring 'treble torments' not
only reminds us that a successful suicide bid brings torments in hell,
but also echoes that moment in V, iii when Lodovico and Gasparo
hurry Vittoria away from the dying Brachiano's side.

So casual seem these parallels, and so oblique their significance, that
they are easily passed over as unimportant. Yet properly understood,
they provide the key to what is generally regarded as the most puzzling
incident in the play. By critics well-disposed towards Webster's art,
Flamineo's mock-death is held to be either an unconsciously ironic
prefiguration of what is to follow or (and the two are not wholly
exclusive) a culminating example of Flamineo's penchant for mockery,
a mockery of the last reality—death.[8] By the more antipathetic, it is
damned as a *coup de théâtre*, a piece of dramatic legerdemain designed
to heighten tension and then bring about a startling reversal.[9] In fact
it is an essential part of the play's thematic and didactic structure, an
incident designed to show that Vittoria, Zanche, and Flamineo are as
deeply involved in evil as Brachiano and his murderers, and will suffer
the same fate. It is, indeed, substantially a re-enactment of the Duke's
death.

[8] See J. R. Mulryne, '*The White Devil* and *The Duchess of Malfi*',
Jacobean Theatre, Stratford-upon-Avon Studies I (1960), p. 208.
[9] See Brown, Revels *White Devil*, p. xlvi.

Though disguised at times by Flamineo's grotesqueries, and by alterations in the order of events, the parallels enforcing such a conclusion
are numerous and close. In the first place the original participants find
substitutes; Flamineo for Brachiano, his simulated suffering recalling
the dying Duke's agony, and Vittoria and Zanche for Lodovico and
Gasparo. Then there are important verbal links. Flamineo's 'I am mix'd
with earth already' (V, vi, 120) recalls Brachiano's 'O I am gone already'
(V, iii, 12), while the Duke's 'How miserable a thing it is to die/'Mongst
women howling!' (V, iii, 36–7) is echoed in Flamineo's comment:

> O men
> That lie upon your death-beds, and are haunted
> With howling wives, ne'er trust them,— (V, vi, 154–6)

The tormentors, too, echo one another. For the terms in which Lodovico
and Gasparo taunt Brachiano (V, iii, 150–4) are very much those later
employed by Vittoria and Zanche:

> [*Flam.*]   Perform your vows, and bravely follow me.
> *Vit.*   Whither—to hell?
> *Zan.*   To most assured damnation.
> *Vit.*   O thou most cursed devil.
> . . . .
> Think whither thou art going.
> *Zan.*   And remember
> What villanies thou hast acted. (V, vi, 121–3 and 130–1)

The last line, of course, echoes Gasparo's words of 'comfort' (V, iii,
142–3).

The parallels go further. Brachiano, as the 'friars' are at pains to
stress, is hoist with his own petard, a poisoner poisoned (V, iii, 155–63).
Vittoria and Zanche taunt Flamineo with being similarly trapped
(V, vi, 123–4), and he, of course, is very willing to agree:

> *Flam.*   O I am caught with a springe!
> *Vit.*   You see the fox comes many times short home.—
> 'Tis here prov'd true.
> *Flam.*   Kill'd with a couple of braches.
>
> (V, vi, 133–5)

There is equally keen irony in the final parallel. When Brachiano
recovers sufficiently to call for Vittoria, Lodovico exclaims in alarm,
'O the cursed devil,/Comes to himself again! We are undone' (V, iii,

168–9). When Flamineo 'riseth', Vittoria and Zanche are left no time to comment. Yet they too are 'undone', and Flamineo with them.

Here, then, is the significance of the mock-death. The events of V, iii prove Brachiano and his murderers hell-bound. In re-enacting the Duke's death, albeit unwittingly, Vittoria, Zanche, and Flamineo emphasise their progress in the same direction. From the first Webster has stressed the commitment of the three to evil. Now we know the price they must pay. 'Trust a woman?' says Flamineo, 'never, never; Brachiano be my precedent: we lay our souls to pawn to the devil for a little pleasure, and a woman makes the bill of sale.'

The final catastrophe

Though Flamineo immediately sees their danger, Vittoria believes, for a moment, that the entry of the 'Capuchins' and their accomplices brings safety. Her reaction when she discovers the truth is characteristic. For her cry of recognition, 'O we are lost', is followed first by an appeal to her captors' pity and then, when this fails, by the guile of 'If Florence be i' th' court, would he would kill me'. This also failing, she accepts the inevitability of death with an attitude of defiance so magnificent that it impresses even her enemies:

> *Gasp.* Are you so brave?
> *Vit.*   Yes I shall welcome death
>   As princes do some great ambassadors;
>   I'll meet thy weapon half way. (V, vi, 219–21)

Unlike Cariola, who fails to match the courage of her mistress, the Duchess of Malfi, Zanche vies with Vittoria in contempt of death:

> *Car.* Thou art my task, black Fury.
> *Zan.*   I have blood
>   As red as either of theirs: wilt drink some?
>   'Tis good for the falling sickness: I am proud
>   Death cannot alter my complexion,
>   For I shall ne'er look pale. (V, vi, 227–31)

Flamineo's response is equally courageous, but lacks that quality of magnificence which distinguishes Vittoria's utterances. At first garrulously philosophical, he goes on to defy Lodovico in sharper and more cynical terms:

> *Lod.*   Sirrah you once did strike me,—I'll strike you
>   Into the centre.
> *Flam.*   Thou'lt do it like a hangman; a base hangman;
>   Not like a noble fellow, for thou seest
>   I cannot strike again.
> *Lod.*   Dost laugh?
> *Flam.*   Wouldst have me die, as I was born, in whining?
>
>   (V, vi, 190–5)

Flamineo then enquires nonchalantly about the make of sword used to despatch him, and encourages his killer to enlarge the wound, while Vittoria taunts Lodovico with

>   'Twas a manly blow
>   The next thou giv'st, murder some sucking infant,
>   And then thou wilt be famous. (V, vi, 232–4)

Admiring her fortitude, Flamineo finds, for the first time, a bond between them:

>   Th'art a noble sister—
>   I love thee now; if woman do breed man
>   She ought to teach him manhood: fare thee well. (V, vi, 241–3)

And in this bond they rise together to what is, poetically, the high point of the play:

> *Vit.*   My soul, like to a ship in a black storm,
>   Is driven I know not whither.
> *Flam.*   Then cast anchor.
>   Prosperity doth bewitch men seeming clear,
>   But seas do laugh, show white, when rocks are near.
>   We cease to grieve, cease to be Fortune's slaves,
>   Nay cease to die by dying. (V, vi, 248–53)

Our admiration for such courage, however, should not be uncritical. It is true that Webster values courage very highly. It is true, too, that he finds it in the bad as in the good. But it is not true to say, with F. L. Lucas, that Webster makes courage the cardinal virtue, the 'first and last commandment'.[10] For it is upon the biblical commandments, upon the laws handed down from God to Moses, that the moral fable which is *The White Devil* rests.

In praising the courage of Vittoria and Flamineo, then, we ought

[10] *Works*, II, 226.

to recognise its nature. 'What dost think on?' asks Lodovico. 'Nothing',
replies Flamineo,

> of nothing: leave thy idle questions,—
> I am i'th'way to study a long silence,
> To prate were idle,—I remember nothing.
> There's nothing of so infinite vexation
> As man's own thoughts. (V, vi, 201–6)

This is the courage of despair, a nihilism born of that state of hopeless-
ness 'beyond melancholy' in which we know Flamineo to lie. This
negative state of mind is revealed, too, when what seems to be a claim
to stoic self-sufficiency is undercut by the admission of spiritual confusion
which follows it:

> I do not look
> Who went before, nor who shall follow me;
> No, at myself I will begin and end:
> While we look up to heaven we confound
> Knowledge with knowledge. O I am in a mist. (V, vi, 256–60)

Flamineo the materialist now acknowledges the existence of a superior,
spiritual order. His tragedy is that he can go no further than this.
Knowing at last that 'This busy trade of life appears most vain,/Since
rest breeds rest, where all seek pain by pain', he is unable to reorient
himself, and dies 'in a mist'.

Inasmuch as she, too, is uncertain of what follows death, Vittoria
is in the same predicament as her brother. Unlike him, however, she is
prepared, as in the quarrel with Brachiano, to acknowledge her sins
and the justice of her fate:

> O my greatest sin lay in my blood.
> Now my blood pays for't. (V, vi, 240–1)

Her final lament, 'O happy they that never saw the court,/Nor ever
knew great man but by report', is not just a choric comment of general
validity, but also a cry of regret at the misuse of her own life.

The criticism often levelled against *The Duchess of Malfi*, that the
retributive action following the Duchess's death is too protracted,
cannot be made of *The White Devil*, where Lodovico and his accomplices are immediately apprehended, and the play ends within twenty-
five lines of Flamineo's death. Yet brief as they are, the play's final
moments do present problems of interpretation. The crucial issue is

how we are to reconcile Francisco's easy evasion of the fate which befalls his followers with the strict retributive schema revealed by the play as a whole. Associated with this problem, and exacerbating it, is Lodovico's suggestion that the murders were committed on the young Duke's authority, since 'thy uncle,/Which is a part of thee, enjoin'd us to 't' (V, vi, 285-6). Taken with an earlier remark by Flamineo, 'He hath his uncle's villainous look already,/In *decimo sexto*' (V, iv, 30-1), this makes us wonder whether his promise of justice is not evidence of his early mastery of the art of deception.[11]

To put Francisco's apparent immunity to justice in perspective, we have to recall the parallel case of Brachiano. Until the end of V, ii, Brachiano's career had seemed to justify the complaints of Lodovico and Flamineo about the ability of the great to evade justice. Yet at the height of his power, at the very moment when his will was being acknowledged as law, he was poisoned. As a result, Flamineo reverses his earlier view that 'noblemen are privileged from the rack', convinced, as he tells Vittoria, that

> If he could not be safe in his own court
> Being a great duke, what hope then for us? (V, vi, 40-1)

The application of this reversal of fortune to Francisco's case is clear. Like Lodovico and Flamineo, we may at first wonder at the ease with which a great man can avoid punishment. Like them, however, we should subsequently realise that all must ultimately suffer for their sins. Though, for the present, Francisco remains a shadowy menace, a symbol of the continuing presence of evil in the world, there will come a time, sooner or later, when events will prove the irony of his contemptuous 'Tush for justice', and he will cry, like Brachiano before him:

> I that have given life to offending slaves
> And wretched murderers, have I not power
> To lengthen mine own a twelve-month? (V, iii, 23-5)

Aware that Francisco's evasion of justice is temporary rather than permanent, we need no longer doubt Giovanni. Young, brave, virtuous and loving, the heir of Isabella rather than of Brachiano or his uncle, Florence, he is a symbol of the regenerative capacity of goodness, as well as a dispenser of justice. It is fitting, therefore, that he should not

[11] For arguments along these lines, see Brown, Revels *White Devil*, p. lviii, and Boklund, *The Sources of The White Devil*, pp. 172-3 and 179-80.

only proclaim his intention of punishing the murderers, but also point out to the English Ambassador, as always our representative, the truth which underlies the whole action of *The White Devil:*

> see my honoured lord,
> What use you ought make of their punishment.
> Let guilty men remember their black deeds
> Do lean on crutches, made of slender reeds. (V, vi, 298–301)

Further Reading

The standard edition of Webster's writings is *The Complete Works of John Webster*, edited by F. L. Lucas (4 vols., 1927). From this edition, which was reprinted in 1966, *The White Devil* has also been published separately (1958). Besides John Russell Brown's Revels Edition (2nd edn., 1966), there is also an excellent modern spelling edition of the play in the New Mermaid Series (ed. Elizabeth Brennan, 1966).

The following books are among those which have contributed materially to the discussion of *The White Devil*:

Rupert Brooke, *John Webster and the Elizabethan Drama* (1916)

M. C. Bradbrook, *Themes and Conventions of Elizabethan Tragedy* (Cambridge, 1935)

U. M. Ellis-Fermor, *The Jacobean Drama: An Interpretation* (1936)

Ian Jack, 'The Case of John Webster', *Scrutiny*, XVI (1949)

Clifford Leech, *John Webster: A Critical Study* (1951)

Hereward T. Price, 'The Function of Imagery in Webster', *Publications of the Modern Language Assn.*, LXX (1955)

Travis Bogard, *The Tragic Satire of John Webster* (Berkeley and Los Angeles, 1955)

Gunnar Boklund, *The Sources of The White Devil* (Uppsala, 1957)

R. W. Dent, *John Webster's Borrowing* (Berkeley and Los Angeles, 1960)

B. Morris (ed.), *John Webster: a Critical Symposium* (1970)

Also highly recommended is a volume devoted to Webster in the series of Penguin Critical Anthologies (ed. G. K. and S. K. Hunter, 1969). Besides a very wide range of critical comment on Webster's plays, it contains a perceptive commentary on the development and present state of Webster criticism.

Index

Aeneid, The, 37
Aristotle, 13, 15, 16, 17, 18, 21

Beaumont, Francis, 8
Bignon, Hierome, 12
Blackfriars theatre, 7
Boaistuau, Pierre, 12
Bogard, Travis, 62
Boklund, Gunnar, 12 n., 29 n.,
    60 n., 62
Bradbrook, M. C., 62
Brennan, Elizabeth, 62
*Brief, but an Effectuall Treatise of
    the Election of Popes, A,* 12
Brooke, Rupert, 19 n., 62
Brown, J. R., 4, 7 n., 19 n., 45 n.,
    55 n., 60 n., 62
Bryant, J. A. Jnr., 10 n.

Cardinal, The, 14
Castelvetro, Lodovico, 17
Catiline, The Conspiracy of, 9
*Certain Elegies done by Sundry
    Excellent Wits,* 7 n.
Chapman, George, 8, 9 n., 10 n.,
    17, 18 n.

Dekker, Thomas, 8
Dent, R. W., 16 n., 62
Discoveries, 13, 15
Donne, John, 17
Dover Wilson, John, 37 n.
Duchess of Malfi, The, 14, 41,
    59

Ellis-Fermor, U. M., 62
Erasmus, 12, 49

Faustus, The Tragedy of Dr., 49
Fitzjeffrey, Henry, 7
Fletcher, John, 8, 18
Florio, John, 8
Fugger letters, 12
Funus, 12, 49

Hamlet, 37
Herford, C. H., and Simpson,
    Percy, 9 n., 10 n., 14 n., 16 n.
Heywood, Thomas, 8
Horace, 18
Hunter, G. K., and Hunter, S. K.,
    62
Hurt, James R., 27 n.

Jack, Ian, 15 n., 62
Jonson, Ben, 8, 9, 13, 14, 17, 18

Kyd, Thomas, 37

Leech, Clifford, 62
Letter Lately Written from Rome, A,
    12
Lodge, Thomas, 16 n.
Lucas, F. L., 4 n., 7 n., 58 n., 62

Macbeth, 37
Marlowe, Christopher, 49
Marston, John, 18
Middleton, Thomas, 14

Minturno, Antonio Sebastiano, 16, 18, 21
Morale Methode of ciuile Policie, A, 17 n.
Morris, Brian, 62
Mulryne, J. R., 55 n.

Parrott, T. M., 10 n.
Patricius, Franciscus, 17 n.
Price, Hereward T., 62

Red Bull Theatre, 32
Revenge of Bussy d'Ambois, The, 10 n.

Sachs, Arieh, 54 n.
Scot, Reginald, 37
Sejanus His Fall, 9
Shakespeare, William, 8, 37, 50
Shirley, James, 14
Simpson, Percy (*see* Herford, C. H.)
Spanish Tragedy, The, 37
Spingarn, Joel E., 13 n.

Theatrum Mundi, 12

Walker, Alice, 16 n.
Weinberg, Bernard, 17 n., 21 n.
Women Beware Women, 14